Armin Kriechbaumer/Jürgen Grünn

Yorkshire Terriers

Care, Training, Diet, Diseases, Behavior

Color Photographs by Monika Wegler
and Drawings by György Jankovics

Consulting Editor: Matthew M. Vriends, PhD

D0451914

Translated from the German by Rita and Robert Kimber.

All inquiries should be addressed to:
Barron's Educational Series, Inc.
250 Wireless Boulevard
Hauppauge, NY 11788

Library of Congress Catalog Card No. 89-38611

International Standard Book No. 0-8120-4406-1

Library of Congress Cataloging-in-Publication Data

Kriechbaumer, Armin.
    [Yorkshire-Terrier.   English]
    Yorkshire terriers: care, training, diet, diseases,
behavior / Armin Kriechbaumer, Jürgen Grünn ;
with a special chapter, the basics of raising Yorkshire
terriers ; color photographs by Monika Wegler and
drawings by György Jankovics.
        p. cm.
    Translation of: Yorkshire-Terrier.
    Includes bibliographical references.
    ISBN 0-8120-4406-1
    1. Yorkshire terriers. I. Grünn, Jürgen. II.
Title.
    SF429.Y6K75   1990
    636.7′55—dc20   89-38611
                                                  CIP

PRINTED IN HONG KONG

5 6 7 8   4900   13 12 11 10

Photos on covers:
Front cover: Yorkshire terrier bitch ''Bloomsbury Miracle of Love'' with four-month-old puppies.
Inside front cover: A boy with his Yorkshire terrier.
Inside back cover: A Yorkie at play. This dog is somewhat too large to meet the requirements of the standard.
Back cover: Three wind-tousled Yorkshire terriers.
Photographer: Monika Wegler

About the authors:
Armin Kriechbaumer and Jürgen Grünn have been raising Yorkshire Terriers for many years with great success and have published numerous articles in periodicals devoted to dogs. Armin Kriechbaumer is the editor of the magazine *Kleinhundewelt* (Small Dog's World).

Important Note:
This pet owner's manual tells the reader how to buy, train, and care for a Yorkshire terrier. The authors and the publisher consider it important to point out that the advice given in the book is meant primarily for normally developed puppies from a good breeder—that is, dogs of excellent physical health and flawless character.

Anyone who takes on a fully grown dog should be aware that the animal has already formed its basic impressions of human beings. The new owner should watch the animal carefully, including its behavior toward humans, and meet the previous owner. If the dog comes from a shelter, it may be possible to get some information on the dog's background and peculiarities there. There are dogs that may, as a result of bad experiences with humans, behave in an unnatural manner or even bite. Only people who have experience with dogs should take in such an animal.

Even well-behaved and carefully supervised dogs sometimes do damage to someone else's property or cause accidents. It is therefore in the owner's interest to be adequately insured against such eventualities, and we strongly urge all dog owners to purchase a liability policy that covers their dog.

Some dog diseases and parasites can be transmitted to humans (see pages 52 to 53). If your dog shows any signs of illness (see page 47), you should definitely consult a veterinarian and, if there is any chance of contagion to humans, you should visit your own doctor.

Contents

Preface

If you are not familiar with Yorkshire terriers, you may find it hard to imagine the contradictory qualities that coexist in these little dogs. They are incredibly curious and eager for fun and adventure, but then again they can take on a self-assured, almost aristocratic air, as though reminding the world that they are to be taken seriously. And last but not least, they have a definite will of their own. It takes loving and consistent training to keep this will from turning into willfulness and obstinacy. Dog lovers forget all too easily that small dogs need schooling and proper living conditions just as much as larger breeds do. Appropriate accommodations are important even though Yorkshire terriers don't require much space and are ideal city dogs. If a Yorkshire terrier feels well taken care of, it will reward its owner with grateful loyalty.

In this pet owner's manual you'll find detailed discussions of everything you need to know to keep a Yorkshire terrier. The authors, Armin Kriechbaumer and Jürgen Grünn, are Yorkshire terrier experts. They have owned and bred these small dogs—which are popular all over the world—for many years. Being active members of a Yorkshire terrier club, they are familiar with all the questions owners of these dogs tend to ask. They explain the origins of the breed and what you should be aware of when you buy a Yorkshire terrier. In the chapter "Training and Everyday Life with a Yorkie" they present many easy–to–follow obedience lessons that help make life with your dog pleasant. The problem of housebreaking, often the first test of the burgeoning friendship between human and pet, is discussed fully here. Another chapter is devoted to the many behavior patterns that Yorkshire terriers have in common with the larger members of their species.

The authors also explain clearly why a proper and balanced diet is so crucial to the well-being of a Yorkie. Grooming procedures, which are indispensable if this long-haired breed is to retain its beauty, are explained step by step, too.

The chapter "Diseases and How to Keep Your Dog Healthy" covers the more common disorders and explains what a dog owner can do if his or her dog gets sick.

The special chapter "The Basics of Raising Yorkshire Terriers" is intended for those who, after serious and thoughtful consideration, decide they want to breed their dogs. In another chapter, readers drawn to the interesting hobby of showing dogs will find the necessary information on what kind of exhibitions, classes, and evaluations there are and what special grooming is required for a show dog.

The suggestions and instructions in this book are presented in clear and straightforward language. As a further aid to understanding, many of them are accompanied by instructive drawings as well as by some fascinating color photographs taken especially for this book by the animal photographer Monika Wegler.

This pet owner's manual will serve the novice Yorkie owner as a comprehensive introduction to these dogs and their care. People already familiar with the breed will find in it useful tips and new ideas.

The authors and the publisher wish to express their thanks to all those who contributed to the book: animal photographer Monika Wegler for her beautiful photographs; artist György Jankovics for his informative drawings; veterinarians Dr. Gabriele Wiesner and Dr. Alexander Hüttig—the former for checking the chapter "Health Care and Common Disorders" and the latter for contributing professional advice on the subjects covered in that chapter.

Some Basic Facts about Yorkies

What Makes Yorkies So Lovable

Yorkshire terriers are undoubtedly one of the most attractive small breeds, and they have all the qualities that distinguish an adaptable yet proud dog.

Toughness, Courage, and Watchfulness are traits that are generally attributed only to working and hunting dogs, such as German shepherds and the larger terrier breeds. Not many people are aware that they are also part of the Yorkie's personality. These small dogs have demonstrated their stamina on many hikes. Walking for 12 miles (20 km) at a time presents no great problem to a Yorkshire terrier in good physical shape.

An Ideal Family and Apartment Dog: An average Yorkshire terrier weighs about 4½ to 6½ pounds (2–3 kg). It is easy to find room for such a small and dainty dog even in a city apartment. A Yorkie can even be left alone for brief periods if it has been properly trained, and its cheerful nature appeals to children and grownups alike.

Because of its independent personality, the Yorkshire terrier easily assumes the role of an assertive member of the family, yet it is not a loner, as is sometimes claimed. The only aloofness Yorkies display is a certain caution, especially after having had some negative experiences—and that, after all, is only right and proper.

The cuteness of the little dogs and the ribbons they often wear—for the practical purpose of keeping the long hair out of the dog's eyes (see page 40)—appeal primarily to women, and we have found that Yorkshire terriers are often bought against the desires of the male head of household, whose wish was for a dog "of decent size." But a Yorkie soon disarms its critics and shows that it is in no respect second to a larger dog. Before long the man of the house is just as proud of the new family member as everyone else.

No Shedding. Unlike other breeds, Yorkshire terriers do not shed in the spring and fall. The few hairs that fall out in the normal course of things are removed with the daily brushing, so the sofa and carpets stay free of dog hair.

The Yorkie Is No Lap Dog

No dog, no matter what its size or breed, is a lap dog by nature. Lap dogs are what they are because of the way they have been treated. How, do you think, would a Bernese mountain dog behave if it were picked up and held in someone's lap all the time? No differently from a small dog. It would develop bad habits and be frustrated because of the inability to satisfy its natural need for movement. It is therefore up to you to treat your dog in a way that is in keeping with its nature.

Proper Breeding Prevents Traits of Degeneration

Yorkshire terriers are small, but they are not degenerate midgets. Breeders in the past have

This Yorkshire terrier is watching attentively what is going on around it. Its hair has been trimmed on both the head and the body to make grooming easier.

Some Basic Facts about Yorkies

worked hard to produce dogs of small size, but the responsible ones among them have always considered the health of their dogs more important than size. There are clear guidelines for breeding Yorkshire terriers to ensure this. A Yorkshire terrier from a good kennel normally lives 12 to 15 years. Unfortunately, the popularity of the breed has turned producing and marketing Yorkies into a lucrative business. To satisfy the demand for especially tiny dogs, ruthless breeders have in the past used smaller and smaller animals for breeding. Isolated instances of this occur even today. The result was that whelpings became more difficult and the puppies born had a shorter life expectancy. In addition, these pop-eyed, round-faced, doll-like little creatures were often hysterical if not downright aggressive.

Origin of the Breed

Yorkshire terriers originated in England, where the breed was first entered in the Kennel Club register in 1886. The Kennel Club is the central organization that oversees all English dog clubs and is the equivalent of the American Kennel Club in the United States. But the history of the breed goes back a long way beyond this official recognition.

For many centuries serfs were not allowed to hunt in most parts of England, as laws dating as far back as the eleventh century testify. To keep them from poaching, the poor were permitted to keep only very small dogs, which, it was thought, would be of no use in hunting. The king's wardens enforced the rules against poaching conscientiously by checking the size of all the dogs they ran across. If a dog was small enough to squeeze through a hoop 7 inches in diameter, it was deemed legal and its master was allowed to keep it.

The serfs used their dogs primarily to keep down the mouse and rat population, but the canines also contributed to the improvement of their poor masters' diet. From time to time, in spite of the laws

against poaching, the dogs would catch rabbits or other small game for their master's table.

Over the centuries a small, robust terrier evolved, a dog that conformed to the requirements of the law but could nevertheless be employed by its owners for hunting.

The Ancestors of the Yorkshire Terrier

The history of the Yorkshire terrier is preserved only in fragmentary form, but we are fairly safe in assuming that the following dogs, now extinct, played a major role in the development of the breed.

The Waterside Terrier deserves first mention. This dog was found primarily in the county of Yorkshire toward the end of the eighteenth century. It was called "waterside" because it roamed along rivers, canals, and the edges of dammed lakes, living on rats it killed and on garbage from the barges traveling the waterways. This short-legged terrier contributed some basic genetic features to our Yorkshire terriers of today, among them the long coat that is bluish with tan markings.

The Clydesdale and Paisley Terriers belonged to the so-called "Scottish terriers." This collective term was first used to describe the dogs of Scots who, during the early days of the industrial revolution (starting around 1785), left the Scottish Highlands for Yorkshire, where they found employment as weavers. The varied terrier breeds were then given the names of the cities where their owners settled, names like Clydesdale, Paisley, and Manchester. The only traits they all shared were their fearless terrier spirit and their long hair. Early in the nineteenth century people began to catalog these dogs and breed them systematically. For many of the workers, breeding dogs was anything but a hobby. Dogs were bred to make a little extra money. That is why the particulars of experimental crossings were not divulged but kept in the family like secret recipes.

Huddersfield Ben, for instance, the dog that is commonly regarded as the progenitor of all York-

Some Basic Facts about Yorkies

shire terriers, was the outcome of a meticulously calculated breeding plan. He was born in 1865 and unfortunately died when only 6 years old, the victim of an accident. In his short life he won over 70 prizes at dog shows, and he scored great successes at the rat killing contests that were then common. He was larger and heavier than the current breed standard (see below) for Yorkshire terriers prescribes.

Yorkshire Terriers in America

We are no better informed about the introduction of the Yorkshire terrier into America and its development here than we are about its earlier history in England. We know, however, that Yorkies have been in America since 1880 and that the breed has steadily gained in popularity. The American fanciers are most interested in very small Yorkshire terriers, and frequently give great importance to coat quality. Though American breeders are, in general, not as fussy about the total number of teeth as are most of the European breeders, they do appreciate "a good bite," meaning level and properly set teeth.

Huddersfield Ben, born in 1865, is regarded as the ancestor of all Yorkshire terriers.

The Breed Standard

To breed dogs of a recognized breed requires the formulation of uniform rules, rules that are put down in writing in the so-called breed standards. A breed standard describes in detail the external appearance and the character traits of the breed in question, and it should be every breeder's bible. Not only breeders but dog clubs, and show judges as well, have to adhere to the internationally valid standards. It is true, of course, that Yorkshire terriers deviating somewhat from the prescribed type can be just as healthy and emotionally reliable as the ones that conform to the standard. But if you think you might want to breed or show your dog, you should buy one that resembles the ideal type as closely as possible. The following paragraphs summarize the most important parts of the standard for Yorkshire terriers.

The Guidelines of the Standard

General Appearance: A lively and intelligent toy terrier, courageous and with an even disposition. Long, straight hair that is parted on the nose and all the way down the back to the tip of the tail. The posture is straight and should convey an air of self-importance. The overall shape should give the impression of a vigorous, well-proportioned dog.

Weight: Must not exceed 7 pounds (3.2 kg). The ideal weight lies between 4 and 6 pounds (1.8–2.8 kg), but a Yorkshire terrier intended for breeding should not weight less than 4½ pounds (2.0 kg).

Size: The standard does not prescribe a size, but dogs of ideal weight will stand 8 to 9½ inches (20–24 cm) at the shoulder.

Head: Rather small and flat at the top; not too rounded. The stop should not be too marked, and the head should not look apple-shaped. The eyes are medium large, dark, and with an alert, intelligent expression. They should not protrude. The teeth should meet in a scissors bite (see page 58), though a level bite is acceptable. The ears are V-shaped and relatively small, in keeping with the overall size of the dog. Drop ears or hanging ears are not permitted.

Body: Compact; short, but not squat. A straight, rather short back is important as are proper angles in the joints of the hind legs, which supply the spring for speedy motion.

Tail: Docked to a medium length, with plenty of hair, and carried slightly higher than the level of the back.

Coat: The quality of the coat is of prime importance in this breed. The coat of the body should be moderately long and perfectly straight, but for older dogs, floor length is desirable for shows. The hair should be silk-like: heavy, smooth, and shiny; never wavy.

Just as important as the texture of the coat are its coloration and markings. The hair is supposed to be a dark steel blue from the back of the head down to the tip of the tail. The correct color has a blue sheen in the sunlight and should be free of brownish or black hairs. The tan on the head should be a rich and bright gold (not reddish gold!). The tan hairs are darker at the root than at the tip. The hair on the head that falls down over the face and is called "the headfall" should be long and of the same rich golden hue. The color is slightly darker at the base of the ears and on the muzzle. The tan on the head should never extend beyond the neck, and no sooty black hairs should be mixed in with the tan. The tan on the legs should not extend above the elbow or the stifle.

According to the standard, woolly hair is a disqualifying defect. Woolly hair looks dull and is very often brownish in color. It is easy to spot because of its much denser growth.

Yorkshire terriers getting their exercise. Yorkies love to romp around in the grass. When running, they can develop amazing speed.

Considerations Before You Buy

Prerequisites for Getting a Dog

Before you introduce this lovable and active little dog into your life, you should be fully aware that you are about to assume a major responsibility. For the 10 to 15 years your Yorkshire terrier is likely to live, it will be entirely dependent on you for its care. If the dog is to be comfortable and happy with you, some basic requirements have to be met.

Not a Toy for Children: Most children long to have a dog as a playmate. But before you give in to their often insistent pleading, ask yourself whether your child is mature enough to deal with an animal responsibly and perhaps to take on some of its care. A dog as tiny as the Yorkie easily gets treated like a toy rather than like a playmate, if for no other reason than that the child is physically bigger and therefore feels superior to the dog. The still clumsy fingers of young children can also cause considerable pain to this small breed. Dropping a Yorkie, even from relatively insignificant heights, can mean broken bones or even death. We advise our readers not to entrust a Yorkshire terrier to a child younger than 10 years old. And if you do get such a dog for youngsters, select one on the larger, more robust side—it will be better able to put up with awkward handling. You should also keep in mind that when adolescence sets in, young people become absorbed in other interests and the time-consuming chores associated with owning a dog— taking it for walks and grooming it—are likely to revert to you.

Not as a Christmas Present: We are loath to sell dogs before Christmas because a dog should never be given as a present to anybody. It is best if the purchase of a dog is planned by the entire family since every member of the family should feel responsible for the dog's well-being. The question of responsibility can be discussed better and with more leisure between or after the holidays.

Time Commitment: If you find grooming a dog a disagreeable chore, you should not get a longhaired breed. It pains us to see a basically beautiful Yorkshire terrier wandering around with its hair matted and all in knots. If the hair of a Yorkshire terrier is maintained in proper condition, brushing takes about 10 minutes a day. A daily walk, some play, and occasional visits to the veterinarian also take time. If you have a full-time job, you should probably not keep a dog at all because the animal needs company and should not be left alone for hours at a stretch. You don't have to talk to it or fuss over it all the time, but it would like to feel that you are nearby.

Housing: Because of its small size, a Yorkshire terrier can be kept in a city apartment without problems. These dogs don't need much space and like to spend much of the time in the family or living room—if they get enough exercise outdoors. Having access to nearby parks or other open spaces is wonderful, and your Yorkie will also appreciate being taken along on excursions to the countryside.

Costs: It is important to give some thought to the expenses associated with owning a dog.

- Purchase price. A Yorkshire terrier from a good kennel is not cheap. You should be prepared to spend about $500 to $850.
- Accessories, including some rather expensive items needed for grooming.
- Dog food. The cost of feeding a Yorkshire terrier is relatively modest and depends on what kind of food you plan to give your dog (see page 44).
- License fees. The fees you have to pay for keeping a dog vary from locality to locality. In big cities they are generally higher than in rural areas. Some few communities have done away with license fees altogether because of the high cost of administration.
- Insurance. It is generally advantageous to purchase health insurance for a dog. But not all insurance companies offer policies for dogs (see Use-

Making physical contact. Even the huge difference in size is no deterrent to the curiosity of these two fearless Yorkshire terriers.

ful Addresses, page 67). Insist on seeing the terms of the contract before signing anything so that you know exactly what costs the insurance will cover. The premiums vary considerably, as do those for liability insurance covering animals (see page 12).
• Other expenses. You have to plan on recurring costs for routine wormings and for other services performed by the veterinarian. Finally, you will have to pay membership dues if you decide to join a Yorkshire terrier club.

Legal Questions Relating to Dog Ownership

As owner of a dog you are obliged to observe certain laws and local ordinances.

Legislation Affecting Tenants: If you rent an apartment or house, you generally have to obtain written permission from your landlord to keep pets. The landlord may revoke such permission, once given, only under exceptional circumstances (for instance, if the dog constitutes a major demonstrable nuisance for the other tenants.

Humane Treatment: Animal welfare legislation, which varies in different localities, generally defines some of the important obligations of a dog owner. Among other things it requires that your Yorkshire terrier

• be housed in quarters adequate to its physical needs
• receive appropriate food and care
• get sufficient exercise
• not be abandoned

Disregarding animal welfare laws may be punishable with fines and even imprisonment.

License Fees: Paying a fee for owning a dog is another requirement the owner has to meet. You have to report the acquisition of a dog—even of a puppy—to the proper authorities within a specified period of time. After you pay your license fee, you are given or sent a dog tag, which the animal has to wear whenever it is not in your apartment or on your property.

Keeping the Sidewalks Clean: When walking their dogs in cities with "poop-scooper" laws, owners have to make sure that no dog excrement is left behind on the sidewalk or on the street; otherwise they may incur sizable fines.

Liability Insurance for Dogs: Even a small dog can cause major damage. It may run across a street unexpectedly, causing an accident, or chew on expensive furniture at someone else's house. As the animal's owner, you will be held responsible for the damage. That is why we strongly advise you to buy liability insurance that covers your dog.

Male or Female?

Many people think that female dogs are exceptionally affectionate and that males tend to be more active and courageous. However, we have never

Different types of hair. The coat of the Yorkshire terrier on the right conforms to the standard. The hair of the dog shown on the left is woolly and thick and therefore harder to take care of.

been able to detect consistent character differences between the sexes in our dogs. What kind of personality a dog develops depends not on the visible traits of the puppy but on how you teach it and treat it.

Female Dogs go into heat (see page 58) approximately every six months and can get pregnant at this time. During the six days of ovulation, when a bitch can conceive, she has to be closely watched so that she will not give birth later to unwanted puppies. The bleeding is insignificant in such a small breed, and some bitches keep themselves so clean that one is hardly aware of their period. If your dog is not so meticulous, you can buy protective panties for it at the pet store.

Pregnancy can be prevented through drugs, sterilization, or spaying. All three methods represent a major interference in the animal's natural life processes. Sterilization—that is, the severing of the oviducts—requires surgery that may not be without danger, and it can lead to permanent estrus. Spaying—removal of the ovaries—theoretically makes more sense because this operation permanently eliminates the sexual cycle. But it seems to us that with a small breed like the Yorkshire terrier it is no great problem to pick up your bitch whenever a male dog approaches when you take your dog out during her critical periods.

Male Dogs are always ready to mate and should therefore also be kept confined if a bitch in the neighborhood is in heat. Many male dogs are remarkably inventive when it comes to finding a way to visit a desirable bitch. If your dog is too obstreperous at such times, you may want to consult your veterinarian. Excessive sexual drive can be reduced through homeopathic medicines. Male Yorkshire terriers also need some extra grooming. Since they lift their legs for marking, the long hair hanging down on the side of the lifted leg gets dirty, and these places should be cleaned with a damp cloth as soon as you get home from the walk. To prevent this problem you can pin the hair up in paper wrappers (see page 64).

Puppy or Full-grown Dog?

A Puppy: We generally advise people to buy a puppy because teaching a young dog is such a rewarding experience. It is exciting to watch the various stages of development. At such an early age, the little Yorkie has a chance to grow into the family and become imprinted by it, so that a close bond is formed.

A Full-grown Dog: If you are looking for an older dog that is already trained, you should make inquiries at breeders. In kennels with quite a few dogs, the breeding stock sometimes gets superannuated. That is why breeders have started occasionally to give up 5- or 6-year-old dogs to dog lovers. Even though these animals have been kept under excellent conditions, they have had to share their keeper's attentions with a number of other dogs. That is why it is easier for them to adjust to a new home than for other full-grown dogs.

Occasionally a Yorkie will become available because illness or relocation forces its owner to give it up. Although such a change is always a major upheaval in a dog's life, a Yorkshire terrier, with its independent character, has a somewhat easier time adjusting to a new family than other breeds do.

Occasionally, a Yorkshire terrier that has had to change owners "forgets" its house training and other schooling for a short time.

A Second Yorkshire Terrier?

A dog does not necessarily have to have others of its kind around. It accepts the human family with which it lives as its pack and forms a deep attachment to its people. In spite of this, dogs like to interact with other dogs, whether in play or playful fighting. Since Yorkshire terriers are so unproblematic to keep, getting two of them may be a good idea if you are prepared to take on the extra cost (such as the higher fee for a second dog) and spend some more time on the dogs. But if you are going to have two dogs, choose either two males or two females. If males and females live under the same roof, you will soon have problems on your hands that you could easily have avoided. When the female comes into heat, there is no way of stopping the male's sexual excitement. The female's period of estrus is one of torment for him, and it is not a pleasant time for the bitch either.

Buying One Dog at a Time requires patience and understanding on your part during the period when the animals learn to accept each other. The less time elapses before the arrival of the second dog, the quicker the first one will get over its resentment and realize that the new dog offers entertainment and company and that it (the first dog) will not be neglected on account of the newcomer.

Getting Two Dogs at Once, by buying two puppies (of the same sex) from one litter, is easier. No feelings of jealousy arise because the dogs are already used to each other.

Yorkies and Other Pets

Puppies get along well with all kinds of other animals. An older dog, however, no matter how good-natured, has to establish its place in the hierarchy of the household. This doesn't always happen without conflict, but the process is different in every case. We used to have Persian cats that were constantly confronted with new dogs, and we were amazed by how harmoniously they all lived together. But be careful if you have small pets, such as parakeets, hamsters, or guinea pigs. Many dogs act on their instincts and regard these animals as legitimate prey. In such a case you have to make sure that the smaller pets are housed in a locked cage and are let out only if your Yorkie is confined in another room.

Advice for Buying a Dog

With Yorkshire terriers it is perhaps more important than with any other breed to consider carefully where you should buy your dog. The popularity of this breed has in the past led unscrupulous breeders and dealers to produce and sell animals without regard for the breed standard and consequently for the animals' health. For the ordinary person it is not always easy to tell a bad apple among breeders. That is why we have included some detailed advice on how to find a healthy Yorkshire terrier.

Where to Buy a Yorkshire Terrier

Your safest bet is to ask someone at the local Yorkshire terrier clubs (see Addresses, page 67) where you can obtain a puppy. The dealers and breeders whose names you will be given are certain to be reputable and reliable. The breed associations keep track of the puppies by registering them in the studbook. Buying from a knowledgeable dealer or breeder also gives you a chance to pick out your own puppy and to get sound advice. The puppies are already vaccinated and wormed, and you receive a pedigree, a vaccination record, and a feeding plan for the first few weeks.

If you answer a newspaper ad, ask in your first communication

• how old the dog is
• if it is healthy and well groomed
• what papers the dog has (see also page 17)

Where Not to Buy a Yorkshire Terrier

Newspaper Ads listing a variety of different breeds are usually placed by shady outfits that mass breed dogs in response to the huge demand for popular breeds. In these so-called puppy mills, dogs are produced continually without regard for the physical condition of the breeding bitches. The innocent buyer then pays good money for a puppy that may turn out quite different from the norm and may have a low life expectancy. Animals from such breeding outfits are almost always physically unhealthy and emotionally unreliable.

Pet Stores and Kennels that display dogs in dirty cages should be avoided. Pity may move you to buy such a dog. If you act on this impulse you are indeed rescuing an animal from wretched conditions, but remember that another one will soon suffer in its place. The empty slot you create will not stay empty for long.

Mail Order Trade in pets is something we oppose as a matter of principle. These dogs almost always come from mass breeding operations as described above. Even if you receive offers to buy through the mail from a recognized breeder, we urge you in the dog's interest to resist. The trauma of being shipped is severe and may leave psychic scars. Any breeder who cooperates with this method of marketing dogs is acting irresponsibly.

Watch Out if You Hear the Word "Miniature"! There is no such classification for Yorkshire terriers. If you are offered a so-called "miniature"

The shape of the ears. The breed standard calls for prick ears (left). Bent or semiprick ears and a thick-looking head (right) are undesirable.

Yorkie, be suspicious. Many dealers and breeders resort to such descriptions in their sales pitch. In most cases they are referring to animals that come from kennels that are intent on breeding smaller and smaller dogs and are doing great disservice to the breed. Salespeople sometimes also claim that short-legged Yorkies need less exercise. This is utter nonsense.

Age of the Puppy at Time of Purchase

Dogs enter a new developmental phase at 9 to 12 weeks of age. They now begin to take a greater interest in the world around them and no longer need constant contact with their mother. At this point a puppy is old enough to change owners. We ourselves don't let our puppies go until they are 12 weeks old because we want to see how they react to their first round of immunizations (see pages 17 and 47). By then it is also easier to judge the character of individual dogs, so that we can better assist our customers in choosing a puppy. For anyone who plans to show or breed dogs later, it is important to know what coloration the Yorkie will develop. This, too, is easier to tell at a somewhat later age. Yorkshire terriers are born black (with tan markings on the face and legs) and gradually change color, a change that does not become apparent until about this age.

What to Watch for When Buying a Puppy

As a newcomer to the dog world, you have no choice but to rely on what the breeder or dealer tells you. If this makes you uneasy, ask someone who is familiar with the breed to accompany you.

• Take plenty of time when buying a dog, and don't hesitate to look around as long as you wish. Good breeders often let their dogs live in the house with them. Our dogs, for instance, occupy the entire basement and have more space at their disposal than we do. Make sure the animals are housed in clean quarters and are well taken care of. This is a prerequisite for good health. However, for reasons of hygiene, some breeders don't allow buyers into the breeding areas. This is something you have to respect. A dull coat, dirty ears, and a sticky residue in the eyes are signs of inadequate care. Slight tearing, which is caused by the long hair hanging into the eyes, is normal, however.

• Alert and curious behavior is the hallmark of a healthy puppy, but don't be surprised if a dog doesn't rush up to you immediately and joyfully. Some animals take longer to respond and approach strangers only hesitantly. Our youngest dogs, for instance, are not used to seeing unfamiliar people. We take them upstairs regularly for grooming but don't allow strangers into the "nursery." Only the older children in the neighborhood—those that have learned how to handle dogs properly—are allowed to play with them.

• Ask to be shown your puppy's mother (the father often is not available because the kennel doesn't own him).

• Look for a silky coat; clear, bright eyes; a straight back and straight legs. These are all important indications of good health.

• Check the dog's bite and make sure that the teeth of the upper and lower jaw meet properly. This is especially important if you may want to breed the dog at some later date. A conscientious breeder will charge you less if a dog has an imperfect bite (see page 58).

• A bloated belly is a sign of worms and suggests that the breeder has not wormed the puppies carefully.

• In a male dog you should be able to feel both testes. Have the breeder show them to you. As a layperson you should not poke around in that part of the animal's anatomy.

Advice for Buying a Dog

Vaccination Certificate, Worming, and Feeding Plan

Puppies are given their first set of immunizations between the seventh and twelfth weeks of age. They are vaccinated against the dangerous contagious diseases of distemper, infectious canine hepatitis, leptospirosis, and canine parvovirus (see page 47). The inoculations are entered in an international vaccination certificate, which the new owner is given when he or she buys the puppy. All future shots your Yorkie receives will be recorded there, too. Check, when you get the certificate, to make sure it has all the necessary information on it, including both your name and address and those of the breeder. If the certificate is incomplete, you may have problems when you want to enter other countries with your Yorkie.

Before you depart, you should also ask if the puppy has been wormed. Wormings are very important.

Most breeders give the new owner a feeding plan for the young dog so that it will adjust to a new feeding routine more easily. A sudden change to different amounts and different kinds of food often causes stomach and intestinal upsets.

Registration Papers

Every purebred dog that was bred should have pedigree papers. This "registration" is a document in the legal sense of the word and belongs to the club that has issued it. After the dog's death it has to be returned to the club.

The American Kennel Club (AKC) registration application must include the name and AKC number of the sire and the dam, information about the puppy's litter, and the name and address of the puppy's new owner. The new owner completes the form by listing two possible names for the puppy, signing it, and enclosing the proper fee. The paperwork usually takes about three to four weeks to process.

Since the litter should have been registered at the time the puppies were born, the breeder or dealer should have the necessary AKC applications at the time of the sale. If the forms are not available, be sure to obtain a signed bill of sale stating the breed, sex, and color of the puppy; the date of birth; and the registered names of the sire and dam, with numbers, if available. This information is vital should you need to contact the AKC in search of your puppy's papers.

If you are buying a puppy from a show-oriented kennel, you may find that the breeder poses some special conditions. In the case of a top-quality animal, the breeder may stipulate terms concerning future mating of the dog. With pet-quality puppies from such kennels, the breeder may agree to sell the dog only if the new owner agrees not to breed it. In the case of a puppy carrying a disqualifying fault, the breeder may even withhold the puppy's registration papers until proof is supplied that the dog has been neutered. The breeder may offer an attractive selling price to close such a deal. In this way the breeder is trying to prevent selected animals from passing along their faults to future generations. Such dogs can still make fine pets! By buying a purebred dog with an officially recognized pedigree, you are refusing to support the mushrooming and uncontrolled mass breeding industry. You are also acting in the spirit of animal protection.

A Bill of Sale

Please insist on a written bill of sale. This document protects both you and the breeder in any legal dispute. Buying a dog is an action that comes under the jurisdiction of civil law. In some states and countries, dogs are still regarded by the law as property in a legal conflict or a claim for damages. A bill of sale can prove useful in a court case if you are asked to give the monetary value of a dog that was injured or killed through someone else's fault. Printed forms are available from breed clubs, but you can also draw up your own. The document should include a description of the dog's appearance as well as the purchase price.

Advice for Buying a Dog

The Purchase Price: We have already mentioned that a purebred Yorkie from a good breeder will cost from $500 to $850. That is quite a lot of money, but you can take our word for it that conscientious breeders don't make fortunes. Yorkshire terrier bitches often bear only one or two puppies per litter, and acquiring a bitch of breeding quality is considerably more expensive than buying an ordinary puppy. Maintaining a kennel also requires a large investment of both time and money.

Essential Accessories for Your Dog

Dog Bed: Your best bet is to buy a cave-like bed made of cloth and foam (see photo on page 28). These beds can be thrown into the washing machine whenever they get dirty. A towel will do for the lining. The conventional wicker baskets are not suitable. They are hard to keep clean, dogs like to nibble on them, and the Yorkie's long hair gets caught on the chewed and split ends of the willow sticks.

Collar and Leash: There are special leashes for Yorkies (see drawing on page 24), which are used at exhibitions and work best for these dogs. They are a little over 3 feet long (1 m), made of braided nylon, and serve as leash and collar all in one. Because of this design they are easy to adjust and take off. A small swivel link keeps the leash from getting twisted and tangled, so that the dog can always move freely. There is also a somewhat sturdier model made of the same material in which the collar is separate. Both kinds are available from breeders or pet dealers.

Another kind of leash is also practical. It is equipped with an automatic roll-up mechanism and gives the dog greater freedom of movement—up to about 12 feet (4 m) if the leash is let out to its full length.

If you want to buy a leather collar, make sure it is not too heavy and stiff. The inner surface should be smooth; felt causes too much friction for a Yorkie's hair. Cat harnesses are not suitable. They are uncomfortable for a dog to wear and damage the fine hair of a Yorkshire terrier.

Food and Water Dishes: If you don't want your Yorkie to shove its food bowl noisily across the entire kitchen floor as it eats, make sure that the bowl has a bottom that won't slide. You can glue a rubber ring on a bowl made of glazed earthenware, stainless steel, or even glass. Pet stores also sell pet dishes with slip-proof bottoms. We put down a washable dish stand for our dogs so that they can't move the food around.

Buy dishes of a size that won't dwarf the small portions a Yorkie gets at mealtime.

Light plastic dishes are not suitable because puppies especially like to chew on them.

Toys: Balls or rings made of solid rubber or latex are best for play. Dogs can pick them up easily in their mouths, but make sure they are not so small that your dog could accidentally swallow one. Toys made of rawhide are also good, and chewing on them strengthens the jaw muscles. Even an old sock tied in a knot will provide a small Yorkie with endless pleasure.

Toys made of light plastic or of material that

A dog carrier. In this type of carrier, a Yorkshire terrier is safe on trips. These carriers are also used at dog shows, where, covered with a velvet cloth, they serve as small pedestals for the dogs to be displayed on.

splinters easily are not suitable. Many toy animals with squeakers inside are also dangerous because a dog can swallow the plastic exterior or the squeaker inside.

Grooming Tools: To do a good grooming job, you will need a wide-toothed nylon or bone comb; a long-bristle brush; a special, cushioned wire brush without nubbins; a mink-oil base spray; and a special shampoo that replenishes the natural skin oils. Because of the particular kind of hair Yorkshire terriers have, the usual dog shampoos are inadequate. You also need a hair conditioner, a clasp for the hair, and some small rubber bands.

Many of these and other items are especially manufactured for this breed and are not available everywhere. Pet dealers are generally happy to place special orders for their regular customers. If you have problems locating a certain item, ask the breeder from whom you bought the puppy or look in dog magazines for advertisements placed by mail-order pet supply houses.

A Carrier Case (see drawing on page 18): It makes sense to get such a carrier if you plan to travel a lot with your dog or if you want to enter it in exhibitions (see page 63). These carriers, with a velvet cloth thrown over them, also serve as pedestals on which Yorkies are presented before the judges (see drawing on page 63). We have also found them very useful for short trips—to the vet, for instance. You can get them in plastic or fiberglass. The plastic ones are cheaper, but they get terribly hot in the summer. Since this is a one-time purchase, we would advise you to get the more expensive fiberglass version.

Food for the First Few Days: Buy a small supply of food before your new pet joins your household. A few small cans of dog food and some dry food will do (see page 44). Most breeders give their clients a little of the food the puppy is accustomed to, since a change of diet at this point almost always gives rise to digestive problems (see page 22). Now all that is left to do is to put down a bowl of fresh tap water, and everything will be ready for the new member of the household.

Training a Yorkie

Helping the Puppy Adjust

Take plenty of time to help your new puppy adjust to its new life. You may want to pick it up from the breeder on a Friday so that you can spend the weekend at home with it. Perhaps you can even take a couple of days off from work after the weekend. This is the time when the dog really needs the attention and affection of its new family. The move means a total readjustment for the animal, and in many ways it is a very confusing time. The puppy is plucked from its pack, which included the breeder's family, and now has to function on its own. Don't try to teach it too much in this phase. Simply give it time to explore its new surroundings. Ask friends and acquaintances to postpone their visits; the noise and confusion created by company are upsetting to a puppy that has just arrived. These are some ways to ease the process of adjustment and to let the puppy get acquainted with its new family in peace.

Important: Examine your home and garden for possible sources of danger (see List of Dangers, page 31) and make necessary changes before the arrival of the new puppy.

The Right Way to Pick up a Puppy

If you have no experience with dogs, have the breeder show you how to carry the puppy properly before you take it home. The way to do this is to put one hand under its chest, support its rear end with the other, and then lift the puppy up. Once you have picked it up, you can carry it on one arm, holding both front paws in your hand (see drawing below).

It Is Wrong

• to hold the puppy in such a way that its legs are bent sideways because the joints of a young dog are not yet fully developed
• to pick up or pull a puppy by its forelegs
• to grab a puppy by the scruff of its neck

Carrying a dog the right way. A Yorkshire terrier fits conveniently on the lower part of your arm. To keep the dog from falling off, the two front paws have to be held together so that the legs are not splayed sideways.

The Trip Home

Try to make the trip, which is the dog's first venture outside its accustomed environment, as pleasant as possible. If you go by car, take someone along so that the person who is not driving can hold the puppy on his or her lap and comfort it. Be sure you have some paper towels and a regular towel in the car in case the puppy vomits out of nervousness. Because dogs are extremely sensitive to drafts, the car windows have to stay closed.

If you drive by yourself or use public transportation, you should use a carrier that can be locked. A tote bag will do, too, but it should never be zipped all the way. Of course you have to make sure the dog doesn't scramble out.

Important: Be careful to keep a good hold on the little Yorkie in your lap during the trip. If the vehicle should stop abruptly, the puppy could easily be thrown to the floor. In a car the puppy should always ride in the back seat.

Training a Yorkie

The First Few Days

Once you arrive at home, the puppy will, depending on its temperament, look around cautiously, curiously, or excitedly and sniff everything. This is how it gets to know its surroundings. Don't disturb it while it is thus occupied, but watch to see if it sniffs in one place longer and more intently than in others. This probably means that it is preparing to urinate. Let it relieve itself on old newspapers at this point. That is probably what it is used to. By no means punish it. At this exploratory stage that reaction would be too frightening. Be patient with the young puppy, even if it leaves a small puddle on your carpet. We'll explain how to housebreak a puppy on pages 23 to 24.

Naming the Puppy: Pick a short name for your puppy that is easy to pronounce and that you think fits the animal. Or you can use the name that appears on the pedigree—but probably in abbreviated form. Breeders often include their kennel's name when naming litters, which can result in long, rather awkward names. An example of this kind from Germany is *Anja vom treuen Freund*. The word *vom* (the equivalent of the English "of") does not mean that Anja comes from a venerable line of noble ancestors but from a kennel called *Treuer Freund* ("Faithful Friend"). Many breeders of Yorkshire terriers like to give their dogs English names because the breed originated in England. Carmardy Little Henry, Macstroud's Soldier Blue, and Craigs Bank Miss Dior are the actual names of champion Yorkies!

Use the puppy's name during the first few days whenever it is time to eat, go out, or play. This way it will quickly learn its name because it associates it with pleasant things.

The Dog's Own Place: From the very beginning your dog needs a place in the apartment or house that belongs to it alone. Usually this is also where it sleeps. Since Yorkshire terriers are by nature curious, they are usually not happy in a corner away from all the action. Put its bed somewhere where the dog can watch everything that is going on but where you won't be tripping over it constantly. Avoid places that are drafty or where the floor is cold. Next to a radiator is not good either because the heat dries out a Yorkie's hair. The ideal temperature for sleeping at night is about 65°F (18°C).

Puppies often choose another spot, separate from their sleeping area, to spend time in. With unerring instinct, most of them make for the place that promises the most comfort and entertainment—namely, the living room sofa. Your dog will be blissfully happy if you let it have a corner there. Put a small blanket there for your Yorkie, for it is important for a dog to find and recognize its own scent. A while ago a distraught dog owner called us and complained that her dog was behaving abnormally. After talking at some length, trying to figure out together what was wrong, we found out that she changed the covers of her sofa very often. The dog was apparently disturbed because it missed finding its own smell.

A Dog Diary: Buy a notebook in which you enter all the important events and dates in your dog's life: vaccination dates, wormings, times of sickness, and medications given. You can illustrate it with photographs so that you will have a visual record of your dog's development. Children especially enjoy this kind of record keeping.

The First Nights

A little puppy misses its mother and its litter mates especially at night. Everyone has gone to bed, there are no new impressions to distract it, and the puppy feels lonely. Some dogs flop down contentedly, go to sleep, and stay in bed until morning, but most puppies voice their unhappiness in disconsolate whimpering and whining. They don't like being left alone. You should have some sympathy for your puppy's state of mind at this stage and move its bed to your bedroom for the first few nights in such a case. This does not mean letting the puppy get in bed with you—just place the dog's bed next to yours. Then you can keep an eye on the puppy and, if necessary, convey a sense of physical closeness by letting your hand hang down without having to twist uncomfortably. An old sweater or a hot-water bottle in the puppy's bed also helps console the puppy for the loss of its mother's body warmth. If you also talk to it reassuringly now and then, the puppy will soon adjust to the new circumstances, and you can return its bed to its original place. When you try to comfort the unhappy little puppy, don't give in to the temptation of letting it get into bed with you—unless you like having a dog there. If you let the puppy sleep with you even once, it may never forget this delightful experience and will try every so often for years to come to repeat it, whining plaintively at night to move you to pity.

Adjustment to Different Food

Sometimes a new puppy hardly eats anything or stops eating altogether shortly after joining its new family. It is so preoccupied with absorbing new impressions that food holds little or no interest. The animal's physical organism is under a lot of strain during these days. There is the stress of adjusting to a completely new life, and on top of that, the food is different. Even the water tastes different. As a result of all this, a puppy will often get diarrhea. In a few cases, puppies even throw up.

In such a situation we recommend a tried and true old home remedy: Give the puppy a lightly salted boiled and mashed potato mixed with some briefly boiled or braised (without fat) hamburger meat. This usually takes care of the problem. You can instead put the puppy on a diet of rice or oatmeal gruel (see also page 50). Do not, however, force it to eat. Just watch the animal to see if it is otherwise cheerful.

If the dog's eyes are clear and if it plays as energetically as ever, the intestinal upset will soon clear up, and there is no cause for worry. If there are other signs of illness (see page 47), you should call the veterinarian.

Teaching the Puppy

Schooling is often considered unimportant for small dogs. Many people don't see the need for dog obedience training because subconsciously they regard such a mite of a dog as incapable of being mean. But anyone who has seen a Yorkshire terrier act the tyrant over the entire family knows differently. Any dog, regardless of its size, tries to exploit its owner's weaknesses to gain advantages, whether it be to sleep on the bed pillow or to beg at the table.

Trying to break an older dog of such bad habits is difficult. That is why you should embark on a reasonable and consistent training program while your dog is still a puppy. Life with a Yorkshire terrier is pleasurable only if the dog is well behaved. What the Yorkie learns during its first six months will shape its character and form the basis of its future development.

In one of his books, the well-known zoologist and dog expert Eberhard Trumler writes, "The success of all training efforts depends on how disciplined we ourselves are. Lack of self-control, inconsistency, insecurity, egotism, and imperiousness are just some of the qualities that inevitably turn any puppy into a neurotic dog." So keep in mind that you are serving as a role model, and act accordingly from the very beginning. Patience, love, and empathy, combined with consistency, are the foundation of effective training.

The Pack Leader: In the wild, the male parent—the alpha animal—assumes the role of teacher of the pups. He instinctively takes a balanced approach to teaching. A domesticated dog, too, regards the family it lives with as its pack and needs a "pack leader." Your family should agree when the puppy first arrives on who will assume this responsibility. Of course, the other family members are indirectly involved in the teaching process too, but they should adhere to the same rules that the "pack leader" follows. If several persons take dif-

Training a Yorkie

Roach back. This flaw can be caused by a lack of exercise. Even a small dog needs plenty of opportunity to run outside.

ferent stabs at training the puppy, the result may be confusion and disturbed behavior. That is why it is crucial that everybody use the same training commands.

Basic Rules for Training

• Try to teach your Yorkie in the context of play. Puppies learn more easily in play situations.
• Don't let any time elapse between a "misdeed" and your reproof or punishment. A dog grasps a cause-and-effect connection only between events that follow immediately upon each other and doesn't know what to make of delayed punishment.
• Use a different tone of voice for praise and for scolding.
• Be lavish in your praise both in words and in gestures, such as petting and scratching the dog. You may even use tangible rewards like a dog biscuit now and then. Pet stores sell extra-small biscuits suitable for toy breeds.
• Don't hit your dog (a light smack with the hand does no harm).
• If your Yorkie absolutely refuses to obey, it is sometimes effective to smack the table with a folded newspaper. But never hit the dog with the paper!

Housebreaking a Puppy

The first step is to find out how the puppy announces that it needs to relieve itself.

Some of the telltale signs include

• turning in a circle
• sitting down repeatedly
• searching behavior, that is, hectic running around and sniffing

If you notice any of these signs, quickly carry the puppy outdoors—to the garden or a street without traffic—and praise it if it does what it is supposed to do. Try to find a suitable spot that the puppy can use habitually and that it will recognize by the smell.

If you are ill or if you are disabled and cannot walk your dog, and if there is no other solution, spread newspapers for the dog on a balcony or in a bathroom. In the case of a male dog, you have to be careful to locate the newspapers strategically. Since male dogs lift their legs to urinate, nearby walls are affected. Small dogs only rarely use cat boxes, and when they do, their digging in the litter is messy. Basically a puppy should relieve itself during its daily exercise outdoors. Take your dog out for a short walk as soon as you get up in the morning and after every meal. Those are the times when it has to go, and this is the best way to get it to relieve itself on a regular schedule.

Pet stores also sell something called "puppy-trainer." The effective ingredients in it are supposed to stimulate the animal to urinate and defecate, thus making it easier for you to train it to use a certain approved spot.

Important: A puppy will inevitably make a few mistakes at the beginning. Punishing it makes sense only if you happen to catch it in the act. If you do, carry it outside immediately and express your displeasure with an energetic "No!" If you wait at all, the puppy will fail to comprehend that there was a connection between its action and the punishment.

Cleaning the carpet after such an accident is best done with some diluted white vinegar or with pure soap. But be careful. Vinegar that is too strong can affect the colors of the carpet. Experiment on a hidden part of the carpet to see what proportion of vinegar and water leaves the colors intact. Vinegar and soap have a strong odor that helps cover up the doggy smell.

If you want to clean the entire carpet, just have it washed. Ask that it not be cleaned with chemicals. The combination of the urine and cleansing chemicals leaves an unpleasant smell.

Our Tip: Buy some small throw rugs for the acclimation period, and place them over the spots your puppy favors for relieving itself. They are cheap and easy to wash. It's best to put a piece of plastic or some paper towels underneath them so there will be no problem of colors running. This makes sense especially if you own expensive carpets.

Getting the Puppy Used to Collar and Leash

You can introduce your puppy to its collar and leash in the context of play outside or indoors. Let the puppy sniff these items first and put the Yorkie leash or a light collar on only for short periods now and then during the first few days. Leave the collar loose enough so that you can slip two fingers between it and the puppy's neck. The puppy will try at first to get rid of this unaccustomed restraint by scratching at it, but it will soon come to accept it.

Practice walking the dog on the leash indoors or in the yard before taking it out on walks. Commonly the first encounter with the leash evokes angry resistance. The puppy will fight the pull of the leash by leaning against it, by trying to chew on the leash, or by simply sitting down. There is no point in dragging the puppy along when it resists this way. You would only cause it physical harm.

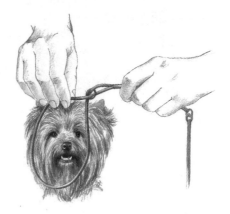

Putting on the leash. In a special Yorkie leash, the loop for the collar can be adjusted so that it slides easily over the dog's head. A small metal sleeve locks the loop in place. The collar should be loose enough for you to be able to slip two fingers between the collar and the dog's neck.

Talk to it encouragingly and praise it if it has made a few steps in the right direction. Once the puppy has accepted walking on the leash, you can begin to take it to busier streets so that it can get accustomed to car traffic and encounters with people and other dogs. Soon the leash will become a symbol for walks and adventure, and the puppy will respond with excitement when you put it on.

Important: Take the collar off your Yorkie after every walk. First of all, the friction of the collar can damage the hair in the neck area, and, second, wearing a collar indoors can lead to accidents. We once heard of a little Yorkie whose curiosity led it to crawl behind a refrigerator, where its collar got caught on the grill. It was stuck there for hours before its mistress was able to extricate it.

The Command "Come"

If you intend to let your Yorkie off the leash now and then in suitable areas where there are no cars, it has to learn the command "Come." "Come" must always have a positive meaning. If the puppy associates anything bad with the word, any further attempts to teach it to obey this command are likely to be fruitless. To call to a dog "Come" and then punish it will confuse it and encourage disobedience.

So praise your puppy enthusiastically if it obeys, and reward it with a dog biscuit. Be persistent if it fails to react because of some distraction. The puppy has to learn to respond to the word "Come" and to its name in any situation. As "pack leader" you have to insist on being obeyed. This is the only way you will be able to protect your dog in dangerous situations, such as in street traffic.

The Command "No"

The command "No" is used to teach the dog that some things are not permissible, whether it be chewing on furniture or shoes or some other bad habit. To make a dog understand what it may and may not do requires absolute consistency. Whenever the dog engages in some forbidden activity, a strict, admonitory "No" has to be issued as soon as you notice the misbehavior.

The Command "Sit"

It is easiest to teach the command "Sit" if the puppy is on its leash. Pull the head up slightly with the leash and push down on the dog's rear end with your free hand. At the same moment, you say "Sit" in a clear, sharp tone and pet the dog if it remains sitting. Reinforce the praise by adding a slow, emphatic "Good dog." Don't work too long on this exercise at first, or the puppy will get impatient.

The Command "Stay"

The command "Stay" tells the dog to remain in place while you start moving away. Teaching it is similar to teaching the command "Sit." Give the command while pushing down on the dog's neck and rear end until it lies down. If it tries to get up again immediately, say "Stay" again and keep it from rising by pushing down on its back.

Repeat this rather complicated exercise two or three times a day and be lavish in your praise. Once the dog has grasped the command, it will remain in a lying position until you release it by calling "Come." Keep practicing, and move a little bit farther away every day until the dog stays even when you have moved out of its sight. Never forget to reward the dog with verbal praise as well as with dog biscuits.

Staying Alone

A Yorkshire terrier can be left alone for a couple of hours a day, and you should get it used to this as early as possible.

Start teaching the puppy by leaving it alone in the apartment for a few moments, listening outside the door to hear how it is reacting. If it whimpers, whines, barks, or scratches at the door, go back in after a few moments, reassure it, and tell it to be quiet. Practice leaving it alone this way every day. If you keep waiting a little longer every day before going back in, the dog will quickly get used to your being away for a short time. Before you leave the house for the first time to do an errand in the neighborhood, you should let a neighbor know that your dog is at home alone. The neighbor can then tell you if the dog remained calm. If not, you will have to practice a little longer to let your Yorkshire terrier develop enough trust to believe that you will return.

Some Bad Habits

Begging at the Table

A Yorkshire terrier can look at you with eyes that will melt your heart, especially if it is begging for food from the table.

If you give in to this look and let the dog have a tidbit from your plate, you will in no time have a Yorkie that makes its presence known with loud whining whenever you sit down to eat. Not only is the noise unpleasant for the people at the table, but food seasoned for human consumption is unhealthy for dogs. It is best if the dog stays in its accustomed place during your mealtimes.

If a Yorkie Chews on the Furniture

Especially during the teething phase (at five to seven months) Yorkie puppies look for things to chew on and may attack your furniture. Reprove your puppy gently but as often as necessary by saying ''No!'' whenever you catch it gnawing at a table leg or whatever. Trying to satisfy the dog's urge for chewing by giving it small rawhide bones or dog biscuits usually does little good. If the dog obstinately disregards your command, you can buy sprays at pet stores that may keep your Yorkie away from objects that are not to be chewed on. Please don't buy sprays that use environmentally harmful propellants.

How a Yorkie Turns into a Yapper

Like all small dogs, Yorkshire terriers have high-pitched voices. This makes their bark shriller and more piercing than that of bigger dogs. How much a dog barks is a question of temperament, but often we unconsciously reinforce a dog's tendency to bark. That is why you should keep in mind the following:

• Don't encourage the dog to keep barking by imitating it.
• Try to avoid noise and hectic activity as much as possible, especially during the adjustment period. Too much action in the apartment stimulates dogs to bark.
• Be tolerant and don't criticize joyful barking during play, vocal response when the doorbell rings, and barking at unusual noises.

If a Yorkie Nips at Pants Legs

Yorkshire terriers have a strong instinct to protect and often think they have to defend their master or mistress even if there is no direct danger. In such a situation they are likely to grab the presumed attacker by the leg of the pants or by the heel. Don't put up with this kind of behavior because you think it's cute, even though the sight of a tiny Yorkie hanging onto the leg of a 6-foot man—obviously an uneven match—may look very funny. Scold the dog firmly if there is in fact no cause for aggressive behavior. If you let it go by, the dog may start to attack any stranger who walks in your door. A dog that attacks without reason can do more than frighten people; a torn trouser leg may cost you quite a bit of money.

Spending Time with Your Yorkie

There are many sad examples of pampered Yorkshire terriers that are condemned by their owners to a ''sofa existence.'' Yet Yorkies are dogs that like to learn and love to get outside and race around on the grass. In the United States, this sporty aspect of the breed has been recognized for decades, and competitions in various physical skills are held in connection with regular breed shows. Jumping over hurdles and retrieving are some of the things a Yorkie is expected to master (see drawing on page 32).

The Daily Walk

Walking with your dog should become a fixed part of your daily routine. Reserve at least an hour a day for it, and organize your time in such a way that your Yorkie gets out into the fresh air three times no matter what the weather is like. Longer,

Two siblings. These 4½-month-old puppies are holding still patiently for the photographer. Ordinarily they are in constant motion, exploring the world around them.

more strenuous walks are something a Yorkie has to work up to gradually.

A dog has to have sufficient opportunity to relieve itself and also needs walks for its emotional health. Sniffing different smells and encountering other dogs are just as important as the physical release of running and urinating.

Walking with a dog can also satisfy important social needs for people. People who live isolated lives find that through their dogs they can easily establish contact with other dog owners.

Watch to make sure that your Yorkie doesn't defecate on sidewalks (see page 12) if you take it walking within city limits or in towns. "Pooper-scooper" laws in many localities hold you responsible for cleaning up after your dog.

Keep your dog on the leash when you are walking along roads. Let it run loose only in safe areas, like parks. Of course the dog has to have learned to obey your commands first, because even here it has to behave properly.

• Don't let your dog relieve itself in places that are off limits, such as playgrounds.
• Watch your dog, and don't let it jump up on or lick strangers. Many people are afraid of dogs and misinterpret even the friendly greeting of a little Yorkshire terrier. The feelings of these people have to be respected.
• Make sure that your Yorkie doesn't overestimate its strength in encounters with other dogs. If a situation arises that might lead to a fight, it is better to pick up your Yorkie. But don't be overprotective. Permit contacts that are not likely to lead to trouble, such as those between a male and a female. Otherwise your apprehensions will communicate themselves to your dog and make it nervous (see page 35).

Yorkshire terrier bitch with her puppies. The dog is guarding her two four-week-old puppies attentively.

Play at Home and Outdoors

A fully grown Yorkshire terrier doesn't play with a toy for long by itself. It prefers to play with someone else. There are lots of ways to play with a dog. You can hide behind a drape and let the dog look for you, or you can throw sticks for it to chase outside. Your Yorkshire terrier will automatically decide what to play. The only thing that matters is that you stay in charge and can stop the game when it's time. You are also the one to control the speed and intensity of the game to suit the surroundings. Horsing around too wildly on a smooth floor indoors, for instance, can lead to accidents if the dog can't brake quickly enough when approaching a radiator or some stairs (see Concussion, page 51).

Taking Your Yorkie Along with You

On Visits: Even if your Yorkie is well behaved at home, it may act in quite unacceptable fashion at somebody else's house, leaping from chair to chair, for instance, or lifting its leg against a tall house plant. The explanation for this behavior is simple: The dog feels neglected and is trying to attract attention. It remembers from its first days with you that people fussed over it when it indulged in such misdeeds. Pay a little more attention to your Yorkie, and let it out now and then if there is a safe yard. If not, go for a little walk with it, inviting the people you are visiting to come along.

Walking in the City: It is probably better not to walk your Yorkie on crowded city streets. Carry it on your arm or in a bag. There are special bags designed for carrying small dogs. These bags are equipped with air holes through which the dog can watch what is going on. Carrying your Yorkie in such a bag is not the same thing as pampering it and is quite useful in this situation. You should also carry your Yorkie if it would otherwise be exposed to a lot of exhaust fumes. Remember that dogs are not permitted in grocery stores even if they are carried in bags. If you plan to make use of public transportation, find out ahead of time if your dog needs a ticket.

Children and Yorkshire Terriers

We have already said that your child should not use or abuse a Yorkie as a toy, but children need more instruction on how to handle dogs.

• They have to know that they must not tease or frighten the dog and must never hurt it.
• They should not bother the dog while it is eating or sleeping.
• They have to learn that strange dogs may behave differently from their own. Especially in the case of tied dogs, caution is in order because such dogs may bite or nip as a defense mechanism.
• After playing with a dog, children should wash their hands. They should also not let the dog lick them, even though the danger of catching anything is minute if the dog is wormed and vaccinated properly.

Going on Vacation with Your Yorkshire Terrier

If you are not headed for some exotic destination like the tropics, it is best to take your Yorkie along. All dogs, but especially puppies and young dogs, are unhappy when they are separated from their family and can't understand why they have been left alone, even if it is only for a week.

What to Take Care of Before the Trip

You will need an up-to-date vaccination certificate (see page 17) for all trips abroad. Check at the consulates of countries you plan to visit to see if any other papers are required. Regulations for entry vary from country to country and are changed frequently. Just about every place requires rabies immunization administered at least four weeks prior to entry. England, Norway, and Sweden insist on quarantining animals for at least four months and are therefore out of the question for vacations. When you plan your trip, you should also find out what inns, hotels, and camping grounds permit pets. Travel offices often have this information available. If you are making advance reservations, ask for a written statement that your dog is included. Many veterinarians and pet dealers have free "vacation planners" to hand out or will provide information on questions related to vacationing with a dog.

The Dog's Luggage

Your dog will appreciate having its familiar things while away from home. So take along the following:

• food and water dishes
• bed
• collar, leash, and grooming tools
• a tag to be attached to the collar with the home address and place of destination written on it
• food—depending on the sanitation in the country you are going to. In some southern countries the tap water is often unsafe to drink. In such a case you should give your Yorkie bottled water (uncarbonated).
• a small first-aid kit with medications for motion sickness and for diarrhea. A disinfecting powder, eye drops, and flea powder or spray should also be included. Your pet dealer or your veterinarian will be happy to advise you on what else you might want to take along.

Car Travel

A dog should always ride in the back seat. Give it a blanket to lie on or, if it is very restless, put it in a carrier that can be locked. A dog should never be allowed to jump around in the car or interfere

Training a Yorkie

List of Dangers

SOURCE	POSSIBLE EFFECTS	HOW TO AVOID
Balcony	Falling off	Dog-proof the balcony. Safety nets are available at pet stores.
Weed killers and pesticides	Poisoning	Don't use these chemicals if your dog uses the garden. Slug bait, especially, has an enticing smell for dogs but is deadly.
Electric wires	Biting through the insulation, electrocution	Run wiring behind the wall, leave no live wires exposed, and unplug wires when you leave the house. Supervise puppies very carefully.
Plants	Poisoning and injuries	Grow no poisonous plants indoors or in the garden—for example, laburnum, lily-of-the-valley, privet, rhododendron, foxglove. Vacuum up needles dropped by the Christmas tree every day.
Broken glass, nails, sewing needles	Cuts on toes and pads and swallowing	Pick up carefully. Don't leave dangerous objects lying around.
Jumping from high seats	Broken bones, possibly even a broken neck	Never leave dog unattended on a sofa or chair when you leave the room. Yorkies like to jump and can't judge the danger of height.
Electric outlets	Electrocution	Equip outlets with childproof safety covers.
Steep stairs, stairs with open risers	Danger of falling, concussion (see p. 51), fractured skull	Carry the dog. Don't let it climb dangerous stairs by itself. Supervise the dog carefully.
Doors	Being caught in closing door; being locked in or out	Watch all doors carefully. Keep them closed if there are drafts.
Detergents, cleansers, polishes, chemicals	Poisoning, internal injuries caused by licking	Store all chemicals in a locked cabinet.

with the driver while the car is in motion. Don't feed your Yorkie too much before you leave.

• Take the dog's water dish and a bottle of clean drinking water along in the car.
• On longer trips you should make rest stops every 1½ to 2 hours so that the dog can get some exercise and relieve itself.
• Make sure the animal is not exposed to drafts because drafts often cause conjunctivitis, ear infections, and inflammation of the respiratory organs.
• If you stop along the way, don't leave the dog locked in the car if at all possible. Especially in the hot summer weather, this can be sheer torture for the animal. In any case, make sure you crack the window enough to allow for sufficient air exchange. Never leave your Yorkie in the car in parking garages, especially underground ones. The high concentration of exhaust fumes there is very harmful.
• If your dog gets carsick easily, you had best give it a pill, prescribed by the veterinarian, before you set out.

Jumping hurdles while holding on to a retrieving stick. This is one of the tests at obedience trials held in the United States for Yorkshire terriers.

Important: Always put your Yorkie on the leash before opening the car doors to get out. It has happened all too often that a Yorkshire terrier—relieved that it can finally leave its prison—has jumped out of the car, run into the path of another car, and been killed.

Travel by Train, Boat, or Airplane

Ask your travel agent or find out directly from the train company, airline, or shipping line how your dog may travel. Most airlines permit dogs in the passenger area if they weigh less than 11 pounds (5 kg). You have to reserve your dog a place when you make your own reservation because the number of dogs permitted on board is limited. Charter flights often have different regulations. If you travel by train, you should take a bottle of water along for the dog as you do on car trips. Dogs often react to boat rides with vomiting and should therefore be given an appropriate drug ahead of time. Ask your veterinarian.

If Your Dog Can't Come Along

Start looking well before vacation time to find out where your dog can stay if you can't take it along.

Relatives or Friends are the safest people with whom to leave your Yorkie. You know it will be well taken care of there, and it won't feel as lost because it already knows its host family. Send along the items of daily life the animal is used to and give your vacation fill-in good instructions.

As a Member of a Yorkie Club you should have no great problem finding another member who will be happy to help you out in exchange for the promise that you will do the same at some future date.

A Boarding Kennel should always be inspected in person before a dog is taken there. The basic needs of the animals are usually taken care of quite well, but there is no guarantee that adequate grooming will be provided. We have heard of cases where the owners found their beautiful Yorkshire terrier practically unrecognizable upon their return because its hair was all matted or had been clipped short.

Understanding Your Yorkie

When your Yorkie nudges you with its nose, whines, runs to the door and scratches, this is behavior that should not be ignored. The dog is communicating with you in almost human terms and could not show you more clearly that it wants to go out. No doubt you know other examples of behavior and emotional expression from your Yorkshire terrier that seem human. The exceptional learning ability of Yorkies and the fact that because of their size these dogs live in close contact with people have added considerably to their range of expression. Still, a Yorkshire terrier is first and foremost a dog—that is, a descendent of wolves, with all the patterns of perception and expression characteristic of canids.

Sense Perceptions

Sense of Smell: The most important sensory organ for dogs is the nose. Extremely sensitive and linked to a well developed sense of taste, it plays the primary role in a dog's perception of the world. That is why dogs try to sniff and smell everywhere. Sometimes they raise their noses high in the air to catch scents there. It is amazing how much information a Yorkie can gather with its nose. It can tell if you are sad, angry, or fearful, what dogs have visited a certain lamp post, and where a spoor leads. Of course, it is also very aware of your particular smell. That is why, when you get a dog, you should not change your scent image for the first six months—that is, don't start wearing a different perfume or switch the brand of soap you use. Give the puppy a chance to get to know your smell first.

Sense of Taste: The only thing we really know at this point about the sense of taste in dogs is that it is closely connected to the sense of smell. The preference for certain kinds or brands of food is no doubt influenced by the smell of the food. The tongue, where the taste buds are located, has two additional functions in dogs. First, because of the tongue's mobility, it is used for drinking; and second, it helps keep a dog cool in hot weather. Dogs have practically no sweat glands and eliminate water by panting.

Vision: Dogs are by nature farsighted and therefore oriented primarily to the perception of movement. To determine exactly what it has caught sight of, a dog needs its senses of smell and hearing. Although Yorkshire terriers have a considerably wider field of view than humans, it is not as large as that of other breeds. For one thing, the Yorkie's profuse growth of hair gets in the way, but the shape of the head also enters into it. A greyhound can even see backwards because its head is so narrow and the eyes are set so far to the side. A Yorkshire terrier has to turn its head a lot more to get a comparable view.

Because dogs have a reflecting layer of cells in the back of their eyes, they can see better in twilight than humans can.

Hearing: Dogs have an exceptionally fine sense of hearing, and they hear a much broader range of

Panting. When excited or after physical exertion, dogs let their tongues hang out. It is typical of Yorkshire terriers to roll up their tongues when they pant.

Understanding Your Yorkie

sounds than we do. Humans can hear sound frequencies up to 16,000 to 20,000 Hz (vibrations per second), but dogs can hear sound frequencies up to 70,000 to 100,000 Hz. That is why dogs can detect not only very small noises from far away but also sounds in the ultrasonic range, which are inaudible to humans. Don't be surprised, therefore, if your Yorkie suddenly acts restless or barks even though everything seems to be quiet. The dog may have heard the family car—which, by the way, it recognizes by its characteristic motor noise—long before the car has become audible to you.

Watch the play of your Yorkie's ears sometime. Seventeen muscles are involved in moving the dog's prick ears so they can tune in on sounds coming from all directions. But the position of the ears also serves to express moods (see p. 34).

Tactile Sense: The only one of the senses that is fairly similar in dogs and humans is that of touch.

Tactile nerves are distributed over the dog's entire body. That is why dogs love being petted and scratched. The most sensitive spots are the front of the nose, the lips, the tongue, and the pads of the feet. Injuries on the soles are very painful to dogs.

Behavior Typical of the Species

Dogs have lived in close proximity to humans for 12,000 years and have learned to adapt and subordinate themselves to man. In spite of this, they have retained many of their wolflike qualities, which are expressed in some basic patterns of behavior that are common to all dogs.

Vocal Utterances

Every dog has a large repertoire of vocal utterances. Whining, whimpering, yelping, barking, and growling describe just a few of the sounds dogs make, and there are sounds between these that contribute to the dog's highly differentiated range of vocal expression. If you listen carefully, you will come to recognize what the various utterances your Yorkie produces mean. Its body language (see below) will help you understand. What is important is how you as its owner respond to your dog's language. A greeting accompanied by happy, excited barking is asking you to answer or to pet the dog to calm it down.

Body Language

The Signals of the Ears: The ears, along with the tail, are the most important barometer of a dog's feelings. You can tell your Yorkie's state of mind by the position of its ears. Most typical for a Yorkshire terrier, and in keeping with its basic nature, are upright, pricked ears. They indicate self-confidence, attentiveness, and watchfulness. Fully alert and curious, a Yorkshire terrier watches all its owner's movements, ready to respond instantly if there is any chance of play, a walk, or something to eat. In a state of excitement, as when you reach for the leash, your Yorkie will look up at you with tilted head as if to ask, "When are we going to be off?"

Ears pointing in a certain direction are a sign that the dog hears some interesting sound coming from there.

Ears folded sideways or backward indicate skepticism, uncertainty, and, if accompanied by growling, aggression.

The Signals of the Tail: Even the docked tail of a Yorkie has expressive abilities. Tail-wagging as a happy greeting is the best-known sign of emotion in dogs. In Yorkies, the entire anterior half of the dog is wriggling back and forth during this ceremony. A relaxed tail, not pressed against the body, expresses contentedness, while a raised tail signals heightened alertness or agitation.

A typical play situation looks like this: The Yorkie stands before you—legs planted firmly on the ground, ears and tail upright—eagerly waiting for the ball to leave your hand so it can chase after it. A tail pulled tensely down, on the other hand, indicates fear and uncertainty. If the head, too, is lowered, this shows a guilty conscience.

Marking and Sniffing

Some parents tell their children, in a simplifying explanation, that dogs "write letters" when they urinate against trees, fence posts, or telephone poles. In a sense this is correct. Male dogs instinctively raise their legs in these spots to mark their territory. They leave behind a "visiting card" and cover up the scent marks other dogs may have left there. It is important that you let your dog sniff to its heart's content on walks so that it won't overlook any marks left by other dogs. This enhances its sense of self-respect. But you shouldn't let the dog sniff in puddles and ditches, let alone on dead birds or animals, because here it might pick up dangerous pathogens (see pages 52 to 53).

Female dogs don't generally leave scent marks, but they are interested—particularly before and during estrus—in the various scent messages males have left behind. Females do not claim territories and therefore don't have to mark. They usually squat to empty their bladder.

Contact with Other Members of the Species

It is always hard to predict what course an encounter between two dogs will take. Much depends on the sex of the dogs involved and on the reliability of their character. Healthy dogs kept under proper conditions respond to other dogs in a natural way, and the whole process follows definite rules.

Dogs that are never allowed to have contact with other members of their species cannot learn these rules. So give your Yorkie a chance to meet other dogs while it is still a young puppy. Not only will the puppy learn quickly how to behave like a proper dog, but each encounter is also an opportunity to find out just how it fits into the canine social hierarchy (see below). During this phase no harm is likely to come to the puppy from other dogs, for dogs obey an instinctive law that forbids them

to bite young animals—assuming the dog in question is not behaviorally disturbed. If you run into a very large dog on a walk you should, for safety's sake, call out to the owner and ask about the animal's behavior. If there is any question, pick up your Yorkie to prevent an encounter.

Important: It is sad but nevertheless true that some owners of large dogs seem to think it fun to urge their dogs to attack smaller ones. This kind of behavior is utterly incomprehensible to us. If you run into this situation, be sure to pick up your Yorkie. Without interference from the owners, dog encounters usually proceed according to the following scenario:

Nose Contact is the first greeting. The dogs sniff noses briefly to find out whether or not they like each other.

The Anal Check is next. Each dog sniffs the other's rear end. Ethologists use the term "anal face" to describe the area lying immediately beneath the tail because the anal glands located there impart much of interest to another dog. Male dogs then proceed to lift a leg so that the other dog can smell their marking scent, too. In the course of this ritual it soon becomes clear how much interest the two dogs have in each other and which ranks higher.

The Ranking Order, that is, the order of dominance, is especially important in encounters between dogs of the same sex. Basically this order is established through the anal check, but sometimes dogs resort to aggressive behavior to clear up any question that might remain. After what is usually a short fight, the weaker animal rolls over on its back and exposes its throat to the stronger one. After this gesture of submission or subordinance, the victor immediately releases the weaker dog. Young dogs, especially, engage in such fights for dominance quite often.

This behavior, which is important to the survival of the species, is, as already mentioned, common to all normal dogs. Overbred dogs or dogs that have not been treated properly and are therefore emotionally disturbed often don't adhere to these instinctive rules of social interaction and sometimes bite even puppies, something a psychologically normal dog would never do.

Digging and Scratching

You may sometimes have observed your Yorkie bury toys or leftover food in the garden and later dig them up again. This behavior, which also goes back to the dog's wolf past, originally had the purpose of building up food reserves and letting the meat ripen. Survival often depended on having meat stashed away for lean times.

If your dog scratches its bed, it is trying to make a hollow in which to settle down comfortably. After scratching, the dog often turns around several times in a small circle before lying down all curled up in a ball. This is also based on a habit that goes way back. The dog's wild ancestors used to stomp down the tall grass to make a bed for themselves. Turning around in circles also serves to loosen the back and get the spine adjusted to the curved position dogs like to assume for sleeping.

A prize-winning male Yorkshire terrier. Four-year-old "My Precious Incognito" has won several championships and is the father of many extremely successful Yorkshire terriers bred by the authors. He has demonstrated his excellent hereditary qualities at many breedings at other kennels as well.

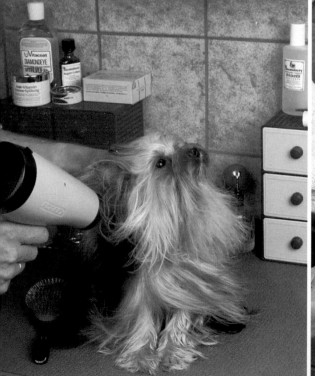

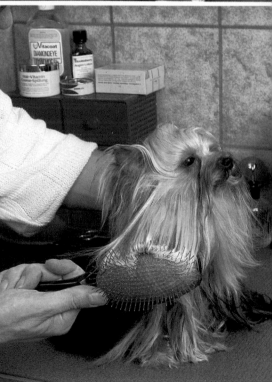

Grooming a Yorkshire Terrier

In this chapter we limit ourselves to describing the most important everyday grooming chores that are required to keep your Yorkie clean and beautiful. If you intend to enter your dog in shows, you should refer to the special instructions given on page 64.

Care of the Coat

The long hair of a Yorkie requires more extensive grooming than the coats of other dogs, a task some people find troublesome. Obviously, a shorthaired breed is less work. On the other hand, you will feel proud when the coat of your little Yorkie gleams beautifully in the sun. To keep the hair of a Yorkshire terrier from getting matted, you must comb and brush it regularly. In the course of a walk or of a wild romp in the grass, knots can form or little twigs get entangled in the hair. If the hair gets seriously matted, the only thing you can do is to cut out the knotted places.

Daily Combing and Brushing

For you to be able to brush and comb its coat, your dog has to stand still in front of you. Most puppies are accustomed to the grooming procedure from their early days at the kennel. If this is not the case, you have to start working on it from the very first day. Place the little dog on a stool or a low table covered with something on which the dog's feet won't slip. A table of regular height is not suitable because the puppy might jump off and hurt itself. It is bound, at first, to try to get away to avoid the inevitable pulling when you comb the hair. Hold on to it in spite of the squealing and

Bathing. After all the shampoo has been rinsed out of the hair (above, left), the Yorkshire terrier is gently patted dry (above, right). Then the hair is dried thoroughly with a hair dryer (below, left) and brushed well once more (below, right).

continue your work. This is the only way the puppy will learn that the discomfort of being combed will be followed by a gentle massage that feels good.

How to Go About It: After you have disentangled the knotted places carefully with your fingers, you start combing the hair, beginning at the tips. Hold the hair close to the skin with one hand and comb through the outermost third of the hair until you feel no more resistance to the comb. Do the same with the middle third, then work your way closer to the skin until the entire length of the hair can be combed through from the roots to the tips in one stroke. After going over the entire coat like this, brush your Yorkie thoroughly. This massages the skin, stimulates the blood flow, and gets rid of loose hair. The dog will enjoy this part of the procedure.

Don't forget your Yorkie's beard when you groom its coat. The beard and the area around the muzzle should be wiped with a damp sponge after every meal to get rid of bits of food lodged there and should then be combed (see drawing on page 43).

Our Tip: There is a special oil for grooming Yorkies that comes in a bottle with a fine spray top. If you apply a little of this oil when you comb and brush the dog, the hair will stay elastic and the ends won't break off.

How to Shape the Hair

The Part: Since a Yorkie's hair is supposed to hang down on the sides, you should take a suitable comb and start parting the hair carefully from the nose to the tip of the tail while the dog is still a puppy.

The Top Knot: The long hair on the head requires special treatment. To keep it out of the dog's eyes, it is tied on the top of the head into a so-called "top knot" (see drawing on page 40). To accomplish this, make a part on each side from the corner of the eye to the ear and take hold of the hair above the parts. Tie it together in a ponytail with a rubber band and a plastic clasp. Appropriate rubber bands and clasps are available at pet stores. Please be gentle and don't pull the hair too tight. Also make sure that no part of the skin is caught, otherwise a bare spot can develop between the ears, and this might be mistaken for baldness or a case of skin fungus. Whenever you work on the head of the dog, watch out not to endanger the eyes.

Our Tip: Not every Yorkie's hair conforms perfectly to the requirements of the standard. The softer and woolier the hair is, the more difficult it is to groom. In such a case or if you simply want to be bothered as little as possible with grooming, you can give your Yorkie a shorthaired look. Cut the hair on the head in cute bangs, and trim the coat on the body about halfway down the legs (see drawing on page 5).

Bathing

You can start giving your Yorkie baths every two to three weeks while it is still a puppy—that

Tying the hair on the head. First the hair has to be parted on both sides from the eyes to the ears and pulled up; then the "fall" can be held together with a rubber hairband and a clasp.

is, from about the fourth month on. It may be better to bathe dogs of other breeds only when they get very dirty, but Yorkshire terriers have hair that is similar in structure to that of humans and should, in our opinion, receive similar care. By using a shampoo that replaces the natural oils, you won't dry out the skin and hair. Don't use your own shampoo on the dog because human skin has a different pH level from that of dogs. You can get shampoos appropriate for Yorkshire terriers at some pet stores and from specialized mail order companies.

The Yorkie's hair should be well combed before you give the animal its bath because knots in wet hair are difficult to remove.

How to Go About It: Plug the Yorkie's ears with cotton wool. Then wet the dog down with lukewarm water. When the hair is thoroughly wet, massage the shampoo lightly into it. Don't forget the belly. Be careful that the hair does not get knotted in the process. Rinse thoroughly, apply a cream rinse, wait a minute or two, then rinse again thoroughly. Start drying the hair with a towel but don't rub. Instead, keep squeezing the towel gently against the body.

Use a hair dryer (not too hot) to dry the coat completely, drawing each strand of hair over the brush as you blow dry it (see photo, page 38). This makes the hair smoother. If you are not used to handling a hair dryer, you can set up an electric heater with a fan and brush the dog dry at a safe distance from it.

Important: Your Yorkie must be completely dry before it is allowed outside again.

If Your Yorkie has Dandruff

Dandruff is the result of dry skin. Floor heating or the wrong kind of soap can cause the skin to dry out. Special shampoos for dogs with dandruff are available at drug stores and pet supply houses. If the dandruff resists treatment, the dog may have hair mites. Consult your veterinarian.

Grooming a Yorkshire Terrier

Care of Eyes and Ears

The Eyes: A discharge collects in the corners of the eyes, especially after sleep, and should be removed with a soft, moistened paper tissue. In addition, check your Yorkie's eyes daily for foreign objects. Grains of dust can easily fly into the eye or a hair get stuck in it, causing eye irritation and inflammation. Remove such objects with a tissue and then squeeze a few eyedrops into the affected eye to soothe it.

The Ears: The hairs that grow inside the external ear should be plucked periodically. Use your fingers for this because scissors are too dangerous. Ears that are very dirty can be wiped clean with a soft, slightly dampened cloth. But please, clean only the external part of the ear! Don't poke around into the ear with a Q-tip. To counteract somewhat the profuse growth of hair on a Yorkie's ears, it is a good idea to shave the tips of the ears about a third down (see drawing, page 65). If you start doing this while the dog is still a puppy, the tips of the ears are less likely to droop later on.

Care of the Teeth

When the permanent teeth begin to replace the baby ones (from about the fifth month on), you should start checking your Yorkie's mouth regularly. In Yorkshire terriers, as in many other small breeds, the new teeth often grow in before the milk teeth have fallen out. The old teeth simply remain standing next to or behind the new ones. Have the veterinarian remove the baby teeth at the proper time.

Another problem associated with small breeds is that they develop tartar more than other dogs. To prevent a build-up of tartar, the teeth should be cleaned about once a week. Get your Yorkie used to having its teeth cleaned while it is still a puppy.

How to Go About It: Raise the puppy's lip and rub the teeth with a soft cloth and a tooth paste (available at pet supply stores). Don't forget the back teeth. When cleaning the harder teeth of a fully grown Yorkshire terrier, sprinkle about half a teaspoon of dibase calcium phosphate (available at drugstores) or some baking soda and salt onto a dampened wad of cotton and scrub with this. Resistant tartar can be removed by the veterinarian with ultrasound vibration while the animal is under anaesthesia. Buildup of tartar that goes untreated can cause gingivitis (inflammation of the gums) and loss of teeth at a relatively young age.

Care of the Paws

After every walk the paws should be checked thoroughly and any small stones, thorns, or splinters removed. If any such objects are lodged in the paws, they cause pain and inflammation or wounds. Superficial wounds can be treated with a disinfectant spray (available at drugstores). More serious injuries require the attention of a veterinarian.

The Nails often grow too long in small dogs because these dogs walk too little on natural ground. Overgrown nails interfere with walking and running. The nails should therefore be trimmed about every six to ten weeks. Watch an expert— your veterinarian, for instance—perform this task the first time at least, or go to a training session offered by a Yorkshire terrier club. There you will be taught how to trim nails and told when it is time to do so. It is easy for a layperson to cut into a blood vessel because it is invisible in the black nail. Bleeding in such cases can be quite prolonged, so you should apply an astringent, such as a styptic pencil, to the cut.

Tips for Winter Care

• Trim the hair between the pads on the feet carefully so that no ice can form there. Use scissors with blunt points. It's too easy to cause injuries with regular ones.

Grooming a Yorkshire Terrier

Cutting the nails should be attempted only after competent initiation. Nerve ends and blood vessels (inset below) are invisible in the dark nails and so are easily injured. Special nail scissors (above) are the proper instrument to use.

• Rub some vaseline into the pads before a winter walk to protect them from the road salt. After the walk, the paws should be washed in lukewarm water, dried, and lightly greased.

• When you are home again, remove clumps of snow that may have formed in the hair, and blow-dry your Yorkie's coat. Otherwise the dog may catch cold.

• A healthy Yorkshire terrier doesn't need to wear a coat in the winter to keep it warm, but in rain and snow it is quite practical to put a rain.coat on the dog. You save yourself the time-consuming task of blow-drying afterwards, and the snow can't form ice clumps in the dog's hair. Use only coats made of a smooth material. Coats made of felt or wool tend to cause matting of the dog's hair.

Cleaning the Dog's Rear End

It is especially important to wipe the rear end of a Yorkshire terrier so that no bits of excrement are left hanging in the long hair. The wiping is best done with a damp rag. If a dog drags its rear end along the ground, this usually means that the anal glands are full and plugged up. Have the veterinarian take care of the problem. Sometimes, though rarely, dragging along the ground can be a sign of worms (see page 52). Take the dog to the veterinarian for diagnosis.

Feeding a Yorkshire Terrier

A healthy diet is the foremost requirement for a healthy dog. Every dog needs food that is appropriate to its physical organism. It needs food that contains the basic nutritive elements of protein, fats, and carbohydrates, plus vitamins and minerals—all of these in the proper amounts and proportions. A dog should never be regarded as a convenient dispose-all for leftovers, no matter how nutritious they may be.

The Feeding Place

In addition to its sleeping place, your Yorkshire terrier needs a spot where it can eat its meals in peace. Set up a feeding place at the very beginning. It represents an important territory for the dog. The best place is probably a quiet corner in the kitchen because the kitchen floor is generally easy to clean. Even if your Yorkie eats neatly from its dish, some of the food may still end up on the floor.

Important: There should always be a bowl with fresh, not too cold, tap water where the dog eats. Remember that dogs drink only when thirsty. When they do get thirsty, there has to be water for them to drink.

Feeding Times

Get your Yorkie used to regular meal times and adjust the number of feedings to its age.

Puppies Up to Two Months Old are fed five times a day: after they get up in the morning, in the middle of the morning, early in the afternoon, late in the afternoon, and in the early evening.

When They Are Two to Five Months Old, puppies get three meals a day: morning, noon, and before the evening walk.

From the Sixth Month On, Yorkies are fed two or three times a day. Late afternoon and early evening are good feeding times. An occasional dog bis-cuit between meals is permissible as long as the total daily ration of food is not exceeded.

Amounts of Food

Individual Yorkshire terriers require different amounts of food depending on age, size, physical exertion, and efficiency of food conversion.

The following amounts are meant only as a very general guideline: A grown Yorkshire terrier weighing 6½ pounds (3 kg) needs about 3½ ounces (100 g) of meat a day (beef is excellent) mixed with 1 to 2 ounces (30–50 g) of dry dog food (use the "professional" meat-and-meal based dry foods—available in pet stores—as they offer a stable mixture from batch to batch). This is the equivalent of about 315 calories.

It Is a Basic Rule that if there is any food left in the dish when the dog is done eating, the portion was too big. If, on the other hand, the dog wolfs down all its food eagerly and keeps licking the empty dish, the amount was too small. Watch to

Combing the beard. After feedings, the hair of a Yorkie's beard should be wiped clean with a damp towel and combed.

see if your Yorkie is getting thinner or fatter. You do this by checking its ribs. If you can't feel them under a layer of fat, the dog is overweight. If the ribs stick out prominently, the dog is too thin.

How to Feed Your Yorkie

According to scientific studies, the ideal dog food should contain 30 percent protein, 5 percent fat, up to 5 percent roughage (fiber), and no more than 50 percent carbohydrates. Add to this 2 percent calcium and phosphorus. These proportions are valid for the diet of all breeds and are found in what wolves, the ancestors of modern dogs, live on. The prey animals wolves hunt are eaten whole—innards, fur, and all—and supply all the necessary nutrients. Muscle meat is rich in protein, the contents of the intestines furnish carbohydrates, and the animal's blood contains minerals. Hair and feathers have a cleansing effect on the intestines. Our dogs, which have no access to natural prey, relieve intestinal discomfort by eating grass.

Commercial Dog Food

If you use commercial dog food, you can rest assured that your dog is getting a good and well-balanced diet. Commercial pet food is composed with scientific precision and subject to ongoing quality control. The laws regulating the production of animal feed are often stricter than those that apply to food meant for human consumption. Check not only the ingredients listed on the package but also the date printed there, which indicates the shelf life of the product.

There are three types of commercial dog food:

Canned Food, which contains about 75 percent water, is available in a wide variety of flavors. It consists of a mixture of muscle meat, tripe, heart, liver, and lung, along with cereals like rice, barley, oats, wheat, and corn. To this are added all the essential vitamins and minerals. Although this type of food claims to be nutritionally complete, you should still complement it now and then with healthy supplements like rice, vegetables, or cereal flakes (see page 45).

Semimoist Food is also nutritionally complete, but it is considerably more concentrated and therefore higher in calories than canned dog food. The moisture content is reduced to about 25 percent, making the animal thirstier. Make sure there is always an adequate amount of fresh water available.

Dry Dog Food is even more concentrated because most of the water has been extracted from it. It contains only about 10 percent moisture and therefore stays fresh for a long time. Here, too, it is important that your Yorkshire terrier have enough to drink, otherwise the kidneys suffer. This potential danger to the kidneys is also the reason why it is safer not to feed older dogs exclusively on dry foods.

Home-cooked Meals

Feeding your dog food you prepare yourself is much more time-consuming but provides a welcome change now and then in the normal eating routine. Of course you have to make sure that your Yorkie is getting all the nutrients it needs. Please keep this in mind, and don't apply your own dietary principles—if you are a vegetarian, for instance—to feeding your dog. The diet of a dog has to be based on meat, which provides the necessary protein. A nutritionally adequate meal should consist of ⅔ meat and ⅓ food of vegetable origin, with supplementary vitamins and minerals.

Meat should never be fed to a dog raw. The danger of salmonellosis, parasite infections, or Aujeszky's disease (see page 50) is too great. Pork in particular can contain the virus that causes this last, serious disease.

• Always boil or simmer meat, but only briefly so that the vitamins are not destroyed.
• Never fry meat in fat.

Feeding a Yorkshire Terrier

• Let the meat cool to lukewarm before giving it to the dog.
• Cut the meat into small pieces. It is easier to digest that way.

Beef, either ground or cut small, is especially nutritious. But you can also use poultry, fish, game, and organ meat like heart, liver, or kidneys. Don't feed the last two too often because they are filter organs and may contain harmful substances. Too much liver also causes diarrhea. Don't give your dog too much pork either, because it is high in fat.

Important: Always use fresh meat to cook for your dog. Old, spoiling meat can cause illness.

Food from Vegetable Sources supplies carbohydrates and stimulates digestion. In this category grain products like oatmeal and cooked rice) are excellent. Vegetables and fruits chopped small— carrots, onions, apples, bananas—are also healthy. Try out different ones and see what your Yorkie likes. Don't give your dog fruit with pits. Quite apart from the danger of choking that the pits represent, these fruits are also hard to digest.

Vitamins, Minerals, and Trace Elements are absolutely essential for your dog's health. Food supplements that contain all the necessary substances are useful. They are available in tablet and liquid form. Ask the advice of your veterinarian or pet dealer. For our dogs, we add about half a teaspoon of calcium and a pinch of salt to their freshly prepared food every day. Contrary to a widespread belief, salt is an important part of a dog's diet, being necessary for the production of gastric juices and for proper nerve functioning.

Some Supplemental Foods should be added to the basic diet. Lowfat cottage cheese is high in animal protein and can occasionally be substituted for meat. An egg yolk twice a week and some chopped herbs (parsley is very popular) and garlic are also healthy additions. Dry bread instead of bones is good for the Yorkie's teeth, aids the digestion, and also supplies carbohydrates. Finally, a teaspoonful of sunflower oil or lard will satisfy the dog's need for fats.

Unsuitable Foods

Try to prevent other people from giving your Yorkie the following foods:

Bones are not good for the small teeth of a Yorkshire terrier. Dog biscuits are quite adequate for keeping the teeth clean. Poultry bones and bones from game are especially dangerous because they splinter easily and can thus cause internal injuries. Be careful to remove all bones from your dog's food and put them in a closed garbage can so that the dog can't get at them. The same applies to fish bones.

Spiced Foods such as sausages and leftovers from your table are unhealthy for dogs.

Sweets are bad for a dog's teeth and cause obesity.

Milk does not agree with all dogs. Many react to it with diarrhea. If this is the case, you should not let your dog have milk. Once they are weaned dogs no longer need milk.

Important Feeding Rules

• Get your dog used to regular meal times and then stick to the feeding schedule.
• Let your dog eat and digest undisturbed.
• Wash the food dish well with hot water after every meal. Dangerous bacteria cultures can develop in dirty dishes.
• Don't leave leftover food in the dish longer than ten minutes; otherwise, in the summer, it will attract flies and get sour.
• From the very beginning, get your Yorkie used to eating everything you give it, including fruit, vegetables, and pills. If you give in the first time it turns up its nose and substitute something more to its liking, you will have a fussy gourmet on your hands before you know it.
• Never feed food directly from a hot saucepan or from the refrigerator.

Feeding a Yorkshire Terrier

• Make sure there is always fresh water in the bowl at the feeding station.

How to Recognize and Correct Feeding Mistakes

Examining your dog's excreta is the easiest way to tell if you have been feeding your dog the right kind of diet. The feces of a properly fed dog are neither too hard nor too soft and are a medium brown.

Constipation, which manifests itself in crumbly feces that are black or show a chalk-like discoloration, is the result of too little roughage in the dog's diet. It can be relieved by stimulating the digestion with linseed, a little evaporated milk, or a small piece of apple.

Eating Feces also suggests that the dog is receiving a one-sided diet. This can often be cured by giving fruit and vegetables, cooked very briefly.

Eating feces can, however, simply be a bad habit.

Diarrhea produces runny feces and can be caused by milk, poultry, or organ meat such as liver or tripe. A sudden change in diet, as when a dog changes owners, can also result in diarrhea. However, diarrhea can also be a sign of illness (see pages 47 to 53). Possible ways to cure it are described on page 50.

Obesity can be corrected only slowly. What is most important is that you, as the dog's owner, remain consistent and reduce the amount of food the dog consumes to about 60 percent of the normal ration. You also have to provide the dog with plenty of exercise to stimulate the metabolism. It is a good idea to ask the veterinarian to draw up a reducing diet for your dog.

How to Keep Your Dog Healthy

Preventing Sickness

Yorkshire terriers are robust little dogs that are healthy and full of vim and vigor if they are kept properly. Keeping them properly means: a healthy diet, plenty of walks, good care, affection, and concern for the dog's emotional well-being. If all this is provided, your Yorkie's resistance to disease will be strengthened. Still, your dog may get sick sometime. As a preventive measure you should take your dog to the veterinarian for yearly check-ups. Keep a watchful eye on your Yorkie so that you will notice any sudden change in behavior. A healthy Yorkshire terrier is characterized by liveliness, a good appetite, a shiny coat, and clear eyes. If any of this changes, it is better to make a trip to the veterinarian that turns out to have been unnecessary than not to go at all.

Vaccinations and Wormings

Immunization is the best preventive against the dangerous contagious diseases of distemper, infectious canine hepatitis, leptospirosis, canine parvovirus, and rabies. In earlier times these diseases used to break out in epidemics, but today there are highly effective vaccines that protect your dog against them.

Puppies receive their first vaccinations when they are seven to eight weeks old. When the next round of shots is due depends on the particular combination of vaccines used. You should be able to determine the date from the information in the vaccination certificate. If not, the breeder or your veterinarian can tell you. It is very important to adhere to the vaccination schedule. This is the only way to insure continued protection. Have all shots entered in the vaccination certificate, so that you have proof that your dog is healthy. This is important for trips abroad.

Wormings should be administered at regular intervals, about every six months. Roundworms and, less commonly, tapeworms (see page 52) weaken the organism's defenses against infectious diseases.

Worming a dog while it is still a puppy (at about five to seven weeks) is absolutely crucial. Even preventive care (worming the bitch before the whelping) and sanitary conditions are no guarantee against puppies being born with worms. Conscientious breeders let their puppies go only if they have been wormed. To be absolutely sure, you should ask the breeder once more about the worming when you buy your puppy. Take a stool specimen along when you take your dog to be vaccinated so that the veterinarian can check for worm eggs. Use only worming medicines that your veterinarian has prescribed, and give the exact dose indicated.

Recognizing Diseases

Symptoms listed below may indicate various diseases and require an immediate visit to the veterinarian. Turn to pages 48 to 50 for detailed descriptions of the diseases and for further symptoms.
- refusal to eat for an extended period
- temperature above or below normal (temperature measured with a thermometer is the only reliable indicator, see page 48)
- diarrhea combined with vomiting and sometimes with blood in the excrement
- vomiting that is frequent or accompanied by fever
- constant scratching, biting, or shaking of the head
- gums turning white
- skin not springing back quickly when it is pinched and pulled up

Important Procedures to Master

Both for recognizing diseases and for treating them, it is important to be able to perform these procedures.

Taking the Temperature: A body temperature of 101° to 102°F (38.5°–39°C) is considered normal for a full-grown Yorkshire terrier. The temperature of young dogs tends to be in the upper range, that of older dogs at the lower end. A temperature higher or lower than normal is a sign of some kind of illness.

Dogs have their temperature measured rectally. Carefully insert a thermometer lubricated with Vaseline into the rectum and keep it there for three minutes. Make sure the dog keeps still during this time.

Giving Medications: Medicines in powder or liquid form, if they have no strong odor, are best mixed into the food. There are various tricks you can resort to if your Yorkie refuses to eat food with medicine in it. Put the medicine into a spoon (powders are first dissolved in water), lift the dog's upper lip on the side, and let the liquid dribble between the teeth into the mouth (see accompanying drawing). Then keep the dog's mouth shut for a while with your hand so that the dog can't spit everything out. Yorkies are very inventive at finding ways to get rid of medicines that taste bad. Another method is to pull the lower lip out so that a pouch is formed, into which you pour the medicine. If the dog's resistance is too great to overcome, you can draw the liquid into a syringe without a needle (available

Giving medicines. Liquid medicines can be dribbled into the side of the mouth between the teeth. In this particular young dog, two upper canine teeth are visible, one of which will have to be pulled.

from the veterinarian) and squeeze it out onto the tongue, preferably in the middle.

Tablets and coated pills are best given inside a little ball of hamburger.

Gelatine capsules don't have any odors offensive to dogs. The Yorkie will usually swallow one without problem if you tilt its head up somewhat and put the capsule way back on the tongue with your fingers.

If your dog needs suppositories, you should have a helper at hand. While one person calms the dog and holds it still, the other introduces the suppository slowly into the anus and pushes it in with a finger as far as possible. Put on a plastic glove for this. Then press the dog's tail against the anus to keep the suppository from being expelled.

Taking the Pulse: A grown Yorkshire terrier has a pulse rate of about 100 to 130 beats per minute. Young dogs under one year old have a higher rate of up to 200. The pulse can most easily be felt on the inside of the thigh.

Dangerous Contagious Diseases

Distemper

Signs of Illness: High fever, a dry cough, diarrhea, watery discharge from the eyes and nose, vomiting.

Possible Sources of Infection: Distemper viruses invade the organism through the body's mucous membranes. They are transmitted from dog to dog or introduced on brushes, blankets, and clothing.

Chances of Recovery: In young dogs, distemper is almost always fatal; older dogs, if they survive, are left with permanent aftereffects, especially to the nervous system.

Prevention: Regular immunization (see page 47).

Infectious Canine Hepatitis

Signs of Illness: Similar to those of distemper. This disease also occurs in a chronic form that has no visible exterior symptoms.

Possible Sources of Infection: This disease is passed on from one dog to another through the saliva or the urine. It can also be introduced through contaminated objects.

Chances of Recovery: Young dogs are especially threatened. There is usually no cure for them once they are infected. Veterinary medicine is sometimes able to save grown dogs.

Prevention: Regular immunization (see page 47).

Leptospirosis

Signs of Illness: The first noticeable symptom is usually a weakness of the hind legs. Further signs are: lack of appetite, fever, increased thirst, vomiting, stomach and intestinal problems, loss of consciousness, blood-colored urine.

Possible Sources of Infection: This disease is caused by micro-organisms called *Leptospira* and occurs primarily between September and December. *Leptospira* are pathogens that are excreted by rats, mice, and infected dogs in their urine. Dogs can pick up the pathogen from contaminated water in ditches and puddles, but also from the scent marks left behind by other infected dogs.

Chances of Recovery: If the disease is caught and treated early enough, dogs usually survive.

Prevention: Regular Immunization (see page 47).

Important: Since some *Leptospira* species are transmissible to humans, scrupulous hygiene is required when dealing with infected animals. Careful washing of the hands, disposable bowls, and the application of a solution containing laundry bleach (see directions on the bottle) to surfaces exposed to urine, feces, or saliva are all recommended. Note, too, that annual boosters are necessary to maintain immunity.

Canine Parvovirus

Parvovirus is hard to diagnose definitely, and it is probably the most insidious of the canine diseases because new strains of the virus keep evolving, strains that are often resistant to the vaccine. Cats are subject to a similar disease, called feline panleukopenia, which is caused by a closely related virus.

Signs of Illness: Serious enteritis (inflammation of the intestinal tract) with frequent vomiting and persistent diarrhea. The runny stool may contain blood, and the vomit often consists of a foamy, yellowish liquid that may be mixed with blood. Apathy, refusal to eat.

Possible Sources of Infection: This disease spreads from dog to dog by way of their excreta, but it can also be transmitted by the owner through contaminated clothes or shoes. That is why breeders who exhibit their dogs at shows fear this disease especially. The virus persistently resists many of the common disinfectants.

Chances of Recovery: Because of the rapid dehydration caused by this disease, a dog can succumb within a few days. Intensive veterinary care involving infusions and antibiotics can save unvaccinated grown dogs if the treatment is initiated in the first stages of the disease. Chance of recovery is better for grown dogs than for puppies.

Prevention: Regular immunization (see page 47).

Rabies

Signs of Illness: Abnormal behavior; in some cases salivating, unprovoked biting, swallowing difficulties, convulsions and paralysis, hoarse voice.

Possible Sources of Infection: The rabies virus is present in the saliva of infected animals (usually foxes) and passed on if the saliva enters the bloodstream of another animal through an open wound, such as a bite wound. The virus attacks the nervous system. The saliva of an infected animal is often contagious before there is any sign of illness.

Chances of Recovery: None. Full paralysis leads to death. The disease can be fatal to humans as well.

Prevention: Regular immunization (see page 47).

Important: If you or your dog have had any contact with an animal suspected of being rabid, you have to undergo medical treatment and your dog has to be placed in quarantine for observation. Re-

How to Keep Your Dog Healthy

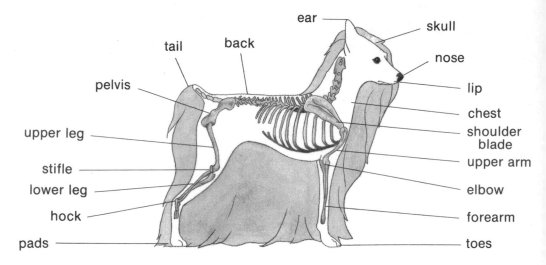

The physical structure of a Yorkshire terrier. The lavish coat of this breed hardly lets you see that a Yorkshire terrier's body is just as handsome and well proportioned as that of many larger breeds.

porting of the disease is mandatory, and health officials have to be notified if there is even a suspicion of rabies. Any animal that is taken abroad has to be vaccinated against rabies. As a rule, the shots have to be given at least four weeks before crossing an international border.

Aujeszky's Disease

Signs of Illness: Similar to those of rabies: restlessness, salivating, and, in addition, scratching, mostly of the head.

Possible Sources of Infection: The disease is acquired through the consumption of contaminated raw pork.

Chances of Recovery: None. Generally a dog with Aujeszky's disease is put to sleep.

Prevention: There is no vaccine against this disease. However, exposure to heat kills the pathogen. That is why you must make sure you feed your dog only fully cooked, never raw, pork.

Common Health Problems

Diarrhea

Signs: The dog's feces are of a soupy or runny consistency.

Possible Causes: Wrong diet; eating snow; bacteria, viruses, or worms; a sudden change in diet; nervousness.

Treatment: In the case of grown dogs, a strict diet is the most effective therapy. Give your dog nothing to eat for a day (depending on the severity of the diarrhea). Replace drinking water with weak black tea with a pinch of salt added to it. The next day the dog should be put on a convalescent diet that might consist of thin oatmeal gruel and zwieback. If the diarrhea persists for another day, you had better take the animal to the veterinarian. Diarrhea not only weakens the organism but can also be a sign of serious illness.

Prevention: A healthy diet.

Constipation:

Signs: Little or no stool.

Possible Causes: Feeding too much meat or too many bones.

Treatment: See page 46.

Ear Infections

Signs: Frequent head shaking, tilting of the head, scratching of the ears, or increased secretion of ear wax. Chronic, untreated ear infections can lead to deafness in dogs.

Possible Causes: Ear mites, bacteria, fungi.

Treatment: Have the veterinarian determine the exact cause and carefully follow his or her directions for therapy.

Prevention: Conscientious care of the ears (see page 40).

Dislocation of Kneecap

Signs: Continued limping, sudden recurrent bouts of lameness. The dog frequently pulls up one of the hind legs when walking.

Causes: Stretched or torn ligaments can lead to dislocation of the kneecap, also called luxation of the patella. In severe cases, the dog is unable to put any weight on the affected leg. Light cases usually don't cause lameness.

Treatment: Only the veterinarian can determine the degree of luxation and prescribe therapy. In some cases surgery is necessary.

Prevention: Prevention is impossible; the condition is hereditary. Although breeders and clubs are doing their best to reduce proneness to it, this abnormality occurs with some frequency in small breeds such as the Yorkshire terrier.

Concussion

Signs: Vomiting, staggering, tiredness, loss of consciousness. If blood oozes from an ear, this may indicate a fractured skull. Epilepsy may be a delayed consequence of concussion.

Possible Causes: Falls, jumping into a table or

Giving ear drops. Hold up the ear with one hand while squeezing the bulb of a medicine dropper with the other to trickle the liquid into the ear. Don't insert the dropper too far into the ear.

other heavy furniture, other accidents, being struck on the head.

Treatment: A visit to the veterinarian is mandatory. He or she has to determine if the skull is fractured.

Prevention: Avoid situations that can lead to accidents.

Poisoning

Signs: Poisoning manifests itself in many different ways, and it is hard to single out symptoms. Vomiting, diarrhea, and apathy can indicate poisoning.

Cause: Ingesting of poisonous substances, such as chemical cleansers, rat or mouse poison, or pesticides.

Treatment: Success of treatment depends on the nature of the poison and on how much has been ingested. If you can answer these questions, it will be easier for your veterinarian to find an effective treatment. If no veterinarian can be reached immediately, you can call the toxicological department of a hospital for advice.

Prevention: Do without chemical pest control in your house and garden. Cleansers of all types should be stored where a dog cannot get at them. Otherwise, close supervision is the only protection.

Heat Stroke

Signs: Accelerated heart beat, rapid panting, lassitude, loss of consciousness. Sometimes accompanied by convulsions. Rise of body temperature up to 107.5°F (42°C). Higher temperatures are fatal.

Possible Causes: Heat stroke results when panting is no longer sufficient to cool the body temperature down. This can happen if a dog is left in a parked car in the sun or as a result of extreme physical exertion on very hot days.

Treatment: Immediately move the dog to a cool place and lower the body by wrapping it in cloths soaked in cool water. On the way to the veterinarian, keep replacing the cloths as they warm up.

Prevention: Don't make the dog work too hard on hot days, and don't leave it in the car during summer weather.

Internal Parasites

Roundworms

Signs: Bloated belly, hiccuping; in severe cases, lack of appetite, convulsions, apathy.

Possible Causes: Dogs get roundworms by picking up the eggs from the feces of other dogs that have worms.

Treatment: Worming. Especially with puppies it is important to adhere to a regular worming schedule (see page 47). After the dog has been wormed, its bed, blankets, and brushes should be disinfected to prevent reinfection.

Prevention: Worming (see page 47).

Tapeworms

Signs: Weight loss; enteritis; muscle cramps; rarely, dragging the rear end along the ground.

Possible Causes: Tapeworms cannot be passed on directly from dog to dog. They find their way to the intestines of a new dog by means of an intermediary host (fleas, lice, mice, pork).

Treatment: There are medications against tapeworms, available from veterinarians, that get rid of these parasites very quickly.

Prevention: Worming (see page 47).

Important: Some species of tapeworms can be communicated to humans. Families with children should be especially careful. If you spot small white segments of tapeworms—the shape of a grain of rice or of a small rectangle—in the feces of your dog, immediately take the dog to the veterinarian for treatment. To be on the safe side, you should see your doctor, too.

External Parasites

Fleas

Signs: Frequent scratching, especially on the ears and neck.

Cause: Fleas suck blood, and their bites and crawling around in the fur cause strong itching. Fleas are usually picked up from other dogs.

Treatment: If your dog has fleas, dust it with flea powder, available at pet stores, applying it against the lay of the hair. At the same time the bed and blankets the dog uses have to be thoroughly dusted or sprayed with an appropriate disinfectant. (If you decide to get a spray, make sure it doesn't contain an ozone-destroying propellant.)

Prevention: There are various kinds of flea collars as well as substances that can be rubbed into the fur to keep fleas off dogs. Ask your veterinarian what he or she recommends. During the summer months especially, you should check your dog for signs of fleas after every walk.

Important: Dog fleas also bite humans, but they usually don't stay long on people. Since fleas are intermediary hosts for tapeworms, you should plan an extra worming after a dog has been exposed to these pesky parasites.

How to Keep Your Dog Healthy

Ticks

Cause: Ticks are encountered with greater frequency in the summer and fall. Attracted by body heat and the fatty acids present in the dog's skin, ticks drop onto the potential host from tall grasses, bushes, or trees and burrow their mouthparts deep into the skin. They start out small, but after sucking themselves full of blood, they can be the size of a cherry.

Treatment: Remove the parasite as soon as you notice it. Do this by daubing the tick with oil (pet stores sell a special tick oil), thus suffocating it. Then you can pull it out easily by turning it like a screw in a counterclockwise direction. Pet stores even sell special tick pincers for this purpose. Never simply pull on a tick. You may pull off the body but leave the head embedded in the skin, where it causes infection. If removing ticks bothers you, you should have the veterinarian do it.

Prevention: Check the skin carefully for ticks when you groom your dog.

Note: In some areas of the United States tick bites can transmit very serious diseases to humans, such as Rocky Mountain Spotted Fever, Lyme disease, and tularemia. Symptoms include fever, muscle pain, and skin rashes. Consult your physician immediately if you have any of these symptoms.

Mites

Signs: Frequent scratching, especially of the paws, arm pits, abdomen, and genital area.

Cause: There are several varieties of mites. All cause severe itching. The parasites are not visible to the naked eye but sometimes can be detected with a magnifying glass as small red or orange dots.

Treatment: Ask your veterinarian or pet dealer for an insecticidal shampoo to wash the affected areas.

Going to See the Veterinarian

Choosing a veterinarian is like choosing your family doctor. Once you have found one whom you trust, you should not switch to another one. The better the veterinarian knows your Yorkie, the better he or she can diagnose problems when they arise.

The Trip: Since veterinarians don't make home visits, you will have to make the trip with your dog. Veterinarians prefer to treat their patients at their office because dogs are better behaved there than in the safety of their home territory. If your Yorkie should be unconscious or severely injured—as after an accident—you will have to place it carefully on its side on a blanket, which is then carried like a stretcher. If the dog is unconscious, be sure to pull its tongue out of the mouth so it will not choke to death on it. In big cities there are animal taxis and emergency transport services for pets. You can call on these if you have no driver's licence. Call local animal protection agencies for telephone numbers.

Rules for Visiting the Vet: Dogs don't like these visits, even if they have had no bad experiences. Be prepared for your Yorkie to react differently from usual.

• Put the leash on the dog before you enter the veterinarian's office.
• Avoid contact with other animals in the waiting room. If you suspect that your dog may have a contagious disease, wait outside.
• Describe the symptoms you have observed to the veterinarian precisely and concisely.

When You Are Home Again: Please follow your veterinarian's instructions for treatment exactly in every respect. Be especially careful to give the right amount of medicine.

Signs of Old Age and Euthanasia

Yorkshire terriers have a relatively long life expectancy and can live up to 16 years or more. To reach such a ripe age, a dog has to have been kept under ideal conditions and received excellent health care. Many Yorkies remain active and lively until they are very old, while others slow down and put on weight. Hearing and visual acuity often decrease. Dogs are not bothered much by this since they rely primarily on their noses, and the sense of smell usually remains intact. In old age your dog's fastidiousness about where it relieves itself may diminish, too, but this has nothing to do with training. Let your dog enjoy the peace and quiet of old age, and take it to the vet's for checkups more often.

Having Your Dog Put to Sleep is the last act of friendship you can perform for your Yorkie if suffering becomes too acute. Please accompany your dog on this last trip to the veterinarian. Don't leave this difficult task up to a stranger. It should go without saying that you will reassure and pet your dog up to the very end.

Being put to sleep is painless for the dog. All it feels is the puncture of the needle, and then it goes to sleep peacefully.

At the veterinarian's. A well-trained Yorkie holds still patiently while its eyes are being examined.

The Basics of Raising Yorkies

Prerequisites for Breeding

Please don't think that raising Yorkshire terriers is simple. It takes time, money, space, and a lot of knowledge to breed a female Yorkie even once. You also take on a large responsibility by letting your dog have offspring. Especially with small breeds, births are often attended by complications that can lead to the death of the mother or the babies. Many people who want to see their Yorkie have puppies "just once" are unaware of this. By the way, the widespread notion that all female dogs should be given the chance to have puppies once is erroneous. People also seldom realize that a single encounter between a bitch in heat and a male dog may result in "breeding." For those with dreams of making money by raising these popular dogs, let them be warned that such schemes practically never work out. A bitch does not conceive every time she is mated and then produce five or six puppies. Two or three per litter is the norm. If, after careful consideration of all the ramifications, you still have your heart set on breeding your bitch, we urge you to take our advice: Join a Yorkshire terrier club. There you have the best opportunity to gather useful information.

Time Commitment: Raising puppies requires quite a lot more time than simply keeping a dog. Even the preparations are time-consuming, and you have to be sure that you will be able to pay proper attention to the mother dog and her puppies. Be ready, in particular, to sacrifice night-time sleep. Our bitches inevitably whelp at night, and if, for once, the birth takes place at a more reasonable hour from the human point of view, it is always on a day for which we had made other plans.

Costs: Dogs of breeding quality are considerably more expensive than regular ones. You have to be prepared to pay about twice the normal price for a good bitch. Add to this the routine expenses of keeping a dog plus various things, such as the stud fee, and costs involved in finding homes for the puppies.

Accommodations: If you live in a house with a yard and with a small spare room for the whelping box, this is ideal. But choose a room where the noise of the dogs will not disturb neighbors or other people living in the house. The squealing of the young puppies and their first attempts at barking can be rather loud. If you live in a rented apartment, you should get permission from the owner or refrain from raising puppies.

Gather Information: The breeder from whom you bought the puppy is a good source of information. Most breeders are happy to answer questions from their clients. Your Yorkshire terrier club (see Addresses on page 67) will also furnish information. You meet people there with similar interests with whom you can exchange information and who will give you tips on what to read.

Important: If you know from the outset that you will want to exhibit or breed your dog, you should buy a dog that already has its permanent teeth. At eight to ten months it is also easier to predict the quality and coloration of a Yorkie's coat. Pick a female that is not too small. A somewhat larger animal can deal better with the physical hardships of giving birth.

The Stud

If you have a bitch you want to breed, look for a suitable male dog in good time. As a neophyte, you should ask your dog club for advice. Even experienced breeders don't find it easy to decide which stud has the best genetic makeup to complement that of a given female. The deciding factor should not be the number of championships a dog has won but the likely quality of the offspring. If a bitch has some flaws, these should be compensated for by the selection of an appropriate stud. Studying pedigrees can be helpful, but if you don't know a

Hair preparation for a show. The hair is wrapped strand by strand in papers (above) and rolled up until the packets are distributed evenly all over the body (below).

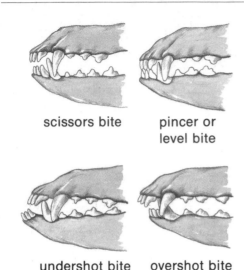

scissors bite   pincer or
level bite

undershot bite   overshot bite

Different forms of dentition. In the correct scissors bite, the upper incisors slide tightly over the lower incisors; in the pincer or level bite, the front teeth of the upper and lower jaws meet exactly; in an underbite, the front teeth of the lower jaw project beyond the front teeth of the upper jaw; and in an overbite, the upper teeth protrude beyond the lower ones.

dog and its character qualities, it is risky picking it simply on the basis of a champion title.

Our Tip: If you own a bitch, don't invest in getting a stud for the first few years, and do without owning one altogether if you are not planning to raise dogs on a large scale. First of all, keeping a male and a female together is problematic, and second, you cannot mate a female with the same male every time. Such steady inbreeding is too risky. You are therefore better off paying a stud fee for the use of someone else's male dog.

Estrus and Mating

Estrus: Female dogs enter estrus (also called coming into heat) approximately every six months,

some only once a year. The period of estrus lasts about three weeks, during which time the bitch is restless and in some cases more affectionate than usual. The swelling of the vagina is the first sign of estrus, and after about four to five days you will notice a red discharge. You should write down this date and count it as day one when you figure out the days on which the bitch can conceive. During this first phase of estrus, the bitch attracts male dogs but is not yet ready to receive them. It is not until the flow from the vagina subsides and becomes almost colorless (the tenth to sixteenth day) that the bitch will accept a male. If possible, take the bitch to the stud to be mated on the eleventh day and plan a second mating for the thirteenth day to improve the chances of impregnation.

The So-called Dry Heat makes it more difficult to calculate a mating date. Here the bitch has no vaginal discharge but is nevertheless able to conceive. If this is the case with your bitch, ask the owner of the male dog if you may leave your bitch there a few days for several matings. The veterinarian can take a vaginal test smear to help determine the correct date for mating.

The First Estrus of a young bitch usually arrives anywhere from the sixth to the eighth month, but the dog should not be allowed to mate at this point. The bitch should be fifteen months old before she is bred. By that time she has grown to full size and is fully mature. But a bitch should not be too old either when she has her first litter. Three and a half to four years is the upper limit.

The Mating: As a rule the bitch is taken to the stud because a male dog tends to perform better in his familiar surroundings. The bitch usually exhibits her readiness to mate a few days ahead of time by moving her tail to the side when she is touched. Depending on their temperament and on how they take to each other, the two dogs will play together for a while before they proceed to mate—if in fact they do mate and one of them doesn't refuse to cooperate. If this happens, please don't get upset. Dogs, like all other creatures, have their whims and peculiarities. If the dogs do mate, the male will remain attached to the female for some time, perhaps as much as half an hour or longer.

Important: Hold the animals in place while they remain locked together after mating so that the male will not get hurt if the female should suddenly twist in an awkward way. Never attempt to pry them apart, but wait until the natural process is completed. Trying to separate them by violence, as by throwing water on them, is cruel and can lead to injuries.

The Pregnancy

How to Treat a Pregnant Bitch

The gestation period of dogs lasts about 63 days. If you start counting from the date of mating, you know when the puppies are due. It's a good idea to write the date down so that you will be sure to get ready in time. If the bitch has conceived, you will notice a slight increase in girth from about the fifth week on. The animal tends to be quieter and more affectionate than before. Don't make any changes in the daily routine. Take her out for walks and fresh air a lot, but don't overtire her. The bigger she gets, the less she should be allowed to overexert herself. Try to keep her from climbing stairs or jumping off chairs when she gets closer to her due date.

The Diet of a pregnant bitch should be highly nutritious and rich in vitamins. At this stage the organism needs more vitamins and calcium, and you should start mixing a calcium supplement or bonemeal into her food from the fifth week on. Increase the proportion of high-quality meat and fresh vegetables and feed the daily ration in several smaller meals. The body also needs more liquid at this stage, and there should always be a bowl of fresh water close by.

False Pregnancy: Even bitches that have never had a litter can have false pregnancies. At first it is difficult to be sure whether or not a bitch has conceived because the behavior and external ap-

pearance are practically identical in a normal and a false pregnancy. But a fake-pregnant bitch often behaves more "motherly" than one that really is pregnant. From about the fourth week after estrus the mammary glands of a bitch with false pregnancy get swollen and sometimes even produce milk, and such a bitch can serve as wet nurse to puppies from an overly large litter or for orphaned ones. If she cannot be given puppies to mother, it is important to provide her with plenty of exercise and keep her busy with other things. She should be fed sparingly. Cold vinegar compresses, applied three times a day to the mammary glands, will reduce the swelling. While a bitch suffers from false pregnancy, she is restless and keeps looking for objects to mother.

Preparations for the Whelping

The Whelping Box: Dogs expecting their first litter should be introduced to the whelping box early on. Place the box in a separate, quiet room and let the bitch sleep in it a few weeks before the puppies are due. The box (see accompanying drawing) should be large enough for the dog to fit in it comfortably. There has to be some room left for the puppies, which will spend all their time in it for

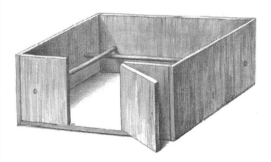

The whelping box has to be large enough. The dowels running along the side walls prevent the mother from accidentally crushing a puppy.

the first three weeks or so. A box about 32 by 20 inches (80 by 50 cm) is large enough; it should be about 12 inches (30 cm) deep so that the puppies will not roll out at first. A little door in one side is practical because it allows the puppies to get in and out when they are ready to start exploring. Inside the box dowels should be mounted horizontally about 2 ½ inches (6 cm) off the floor and 1 ½ inches (4 cm) from the walls so that the bitch will not accidentally squash the puppies. This way the puppies can get out of the way if their mother lies down too close to the side of the box.

The bottom of the box can be lined with a thick layer of newspapers and clean towels on top.

Getting Ready for the Birth: About two weeks before the due date, you should let your veterinarian know when your dog is expecting and ask if you could, in an emergency, get in touch outside of office hours, perhaps even at night. The dog should have been wormed about four weeks before the expected birth. Two days before the due date, the whelping box and its surroundings should be disinfected. Then you should get the animal ready: The hair should be put up in wrappers (see page 64) or cut so that no puppy can accidentally strangle in a strand of long hair. Carefully shave the bitch's abdomen to expose the teats.

Things to Have at Hand: The last act of preparation is to get the following ready: additional towels, bandaging materials in case something goes wrong, thread and scissors to tie off the umbilical cord, a disinfectant spray, a thermometer, and a scale for weighing.

The Whelping

As early as 24 to 36 hours before the birth there is a first sign, a drop in body temperature to 98.5°F (37°C). If you take your dog's temperature regularly from the fifty-seventh day of pregnancy on, you will probably be able to predict when the puppies will arrive. Immediately before the birth, the temperature rises back to normal. Before the labor pains begin, the bitch starts to pant, practically stops eating, and gets restless. It may still take hours after this initial phase before the puppies are born. Make sure during this time that the room with the whelping box is about 72°F (22°C). The bitch should have a familiar person around to soothe her.

The Birth: After the contractions have become more frequent, a liquid is discharged from the vagina, and soon after that the grayish blue amniotic sac with the first puppy in it becomes visible and is pushed out by strong muscle contractions. The rest of the puppies usually appear at intervals of a quarter to a half hour. Watch to make sure that the afterbirth is expelled after every puppy. If it stays inside the mother, it leads to poisoning. If all goes normally, the bitch, obeying instinct, tears open the amniotic sac and diligently licks the newborn dry. She also bites off the umbilical cord and eats part of the afterbirth. But sometimes she is too exhausted or distracted by the birth of the next puppy. In that case you have to help out with these most important tasks.

• To free the puppy as quickly as possible so that it can breathe, you tear open the amniotic sac near the head and clean the puppy's head and nose. Also clear the inside of the mouth of mucus.

• Rub the puppy dry vigorously with a towel. You don't have to be overly gentle—the mother does it quite roughly too—because the circulation is stimulated by the rubbing.

• The first squeaking is a sign that the puppy has gotten enough air to breathe. Now you can put it down near its mother's teats, where it would normally scrabble on its own, guided by sure instinct. To help it drink you can push the teat into its mouth and lay its front paws against the mother's belly.

• If the bitch should neglect to bite off the umbilical cord, you should tie it off close to the puppy's belly and cut it about ½ inch (1 cm) away from the tied place. The piece of umbilical cord that is left will dry out and fall off later.

Complications: Situations can arise during any whelping that call for skills that are beyond a be-

The Basics of Raising Yorkies

When nursing, the puppies push against the mother's belly with their paws, thus stimulating the milk flow.

ginner. Maybe no puppy appears in spite of the contractions, or the amniotic sac breaks in the birth canal so that the puppy has to be gotten out as quickly as possible, or the puppy fails to breathe properly once it is born. Possibly a Caesarean section will have to be considered. Because of such potential complications, we advise you to get the help of an experienced breeder for your bitch's first whelping. A breeder knows best when it's time to call the veterinarian.

The Bitch and Her Puppies during the First Three Weeks

A healthy bitch looks after her puppies for the first three weeks without any outside help. She feeds and cares for them and keeps the bed clean by eating the puppies' feces. The puppies are blind for the first ten days and don't hear until the twelfth day. But their sense of smell always guides them to their source of nourishment. With their paws they push against or knead the mother's belly, thus stimulating the flow of milk. All you have to do normally—apart from watching—is to keep the room temperature at around 68°F (20°C), keep out drafts, and change the towels in the whelping box periodically.

The Temperature inside the whelping box has to remain steady for the first two weeks. This can be done by suspending a heat lamp at the proper height above the box. However, we always use a small electric heating pad, on top of which we spread a couple of towels and a blanket for insulation. The heating pad has to have a thermostat so that it doesn't get too hot. You also have to make sure the mother dog doesn't chew on the electric wire.

If the Bitch Doesn't Have Enough Milk: When that happens, we feed the puppies a combination of ⅓ cream (10 percent fat) and ⅔ scalded whole milk. You can also feed them puppy formula (dry milk), available from pet stores, your veterinarian, or some drugstores. There are special bottles for bottlefeeding, also available at pet stores. The puppies should get fed about every two hours. You may be able to find another bitch through your Yorkie club to act as wet nurse for the puppies. The nursing mother should get plenty of extra nutritious food during this period because the physical demands that are made on her body are great. Excellent supplements to her diet at this point are cottage cheese, some honey, calcium, and an egg yolk now and then. Try to disturb the mother and her babies as little as possible, and tell your friends who will want to admire the puppies that they will have to wait a bit. The risk that strangers might accidentally introduce bacteria or parasites is too great.

Complications: During the first two weeks, the bitch may develop a mineral imbalance because nursing deprives her body of so much calcium. The condition makes itself manifest through restlessness and violent trembling, leading up to an attack of convulsions, called eclampsia. You have to call the veterinarian as soon as you notice the first signs, because only he or she can save the animal by giving it a calcium shot.

Development of the Puppies

After spending the first three weeks of their lives mostly sleeping and nursing, the puppies are now ready for their first wobbling attempts at locomotion and exploration. They leave their box more and more often to investigate the room they are in. At about six weeks, they are weaned. This marks the beginning of the most important phase in their development, the so-called imprinting phase. They begin to discover themselves, others of their own kind, and humans. All the impressions they receive and the social contacts they have during this phase affect their later behavior. It is very important that you spend time with the puppies now. The more you play with them, touch them, talk to them, the more trust they will develop and the closer a bond they will be able to form to humans. Specialists in animal behavior use the term "socialization phase" for weeks eight to twelve. During this time the puppies learn to distinguish between play and seriousness. They test various kinds of social behavior in tussles with their litter mates and try out different kinds of expressive behavior, ranging from threatening stances to gestures of affection. The mother dog supervises and bats them now and then if they get too wild. This is the time when their eagerness to learn is at a peak and when you should start training the puppies.

Feeding the Puppies

For the First Four Weeks or so, the puppies need only their mother's milk. Then you should start giving them additional food, at first two to three times a day. We give our puppies the milk mixture mentioned earlier along with some hamburger meat, rolled oats, and calcium and vitamin supplements. For a change you can add some fructose or honey. Commercial puppy food is also very good, and we have had good experiences using baby foods, such as beef, veal, or poultry with vegetables.

From the Sixth Week on, the puppies should get four to five meals a day consisting of more solid food. The commercial canned puppy foods contain all the necessary nutrients.

Important: The chunks of meat in canned dog food are usually too big for little puppies, so you should break them up. With a potato masher you can reduce the stuff to a good consistency.

Taking Your Yorkie to a Show

The Purpose of Dog Shows

At shows, dogs are evaluated by judges in terms of their external appearance and their stance and movements on the exhibition bench. The breed standard serves as the basis for the judge's decisions. The avowed purpose of dog shows is to improve the breed and to check the quality of the breeding stock. Although there is much talk of "competition for beauty," the main concern is to keep the breed healthy. When you see all the Yorkshire terriers, their long hair styled to show them off to best advantage, you may have some justifiable doubts. But consider: The ribbon has the purpose of keeping the hair out of the dog's face, and the colorful velvet pedestal serves to show off this small dog better. Walking properly on the leash and general obedience are also taken into account and are skills that one should be able to take for granted

Presentation at an exhibition. It takes a lot of patience, practice, and persistence to get a Yorkie ready to pose perfectly before a judge.

in any dog. Another reason, and not an insignificant one, for showing one's dog at exhibitions is of potential economic importance. Not infrequently insurance companies turn to exhibition judges or dog clubs to get a monetary estimate of what a dog was worth. In the absence of a show evaluation, insurance companies often reimburse the owner only for part of the cost of replacement, that is, for less than the price of a new puppy. What sentimental value the animal had for its owner is not even taken into consideration.

Assignment to Classes and Evaluation at Dog Shows

The Assignment to a Class at a dog show is based on the age of a dog and the titles it has already won:

• The youngest class, the Puppy Class is for dogs six months to one year old. The Puppy Class is limited to dogs whelped in the United States and Canada.
• The Novice Class (six months or older), is open to dogs that have never won a first prize in any class other than puppy class, and have won fewer than three first prizes in the novice class itself. The class is limited to dogs whelped in the United States and Canada.
• Bred by Exhibitor Class is open to all dogs six months of age or older (except champions) exhibited by the breeder (or the breeder's immediate family) as listed in the records of the AKC.
• American Bred Class is open to dogs six months of age or older (except champions) bred and whelped in the United States.
• Open Class is open to all dogs six months of age or older. There are no exceptions.

Evaluation Grades: Every dog that enters a show is given an evaluation grade and a brief judge's report:

Taking Your Yorkie to a Show

Grooming for an exhibition. A Yorkie looks neater if the hair on the upper third of the ears is removed with special battery-powered clippers.

• The grade "excellent" may be awarded only to a dog that conforms very closely to the breed standard, demonstrates a calm nature, and displays a flawless posture.
• The grade "very good" describes the same qualities but allows for a few minor flaws.
• The grade "good" is used for dogs that display the traits of their breed but do have defects.
• "Satisfactory" is the term applied to dogs whose appearance doesn't quite match the breed standard or whose physical condition leaves something to be desired.

Prerequisites for Entering a Dog in a Show

Exhibitions are organized differently in different parts of the world; and, depending on the size of the show and the kind of organizing body and participants, a variety of evaluation categories, titles, and championships are awarded.

If you are thinking of showing your Yorkie for the first time, your best bet is a "special breed show." As a beginner, you will find your way around more easily in these smaller, more surveyable shows. The atmosphere is usually more informal than at big shows, and it is easier to get into conversation with other exhibitors.

First go to a show as a visitor, admire the beautiful animals, and familiarize yourself with how everything is done. (By the way, you don't have to own a dog to visit dog shows.) The people showing dogs will gladly answer your questions—unless they happen to be busy getting their dog ready for display. Your club can tell you when and where various shows are held. In order to participate in a show you will need to do the following:

• Apply in good time. You can get application forms through your club. The form asks for the names of the dog and of its parents, your dog's studbook number, the litter's date of birth, and the names and addresses of the owner and the breeder. You are also asked to indicate the class in which you wish to enter your dog (see page 63).
• Pay the application fee, which will vary in amount depending on the particular show and the dog's class.
• Supply the dog's pedigree and its international vaccination certificate.

Grooming a Show Dog

You will have to spend extra time and effort grooming your Yorkie if you wish to present it at an exhibition. An unkempt dog is a discourtesy to the judge who is expected to evaluate the animal.

Putting the Yorkie's Hair Up

In judging Yorkshire terriers, what is considered especially important, apart from a healthy anatomy, is the condition of the coat. This is why you should treat it with special care. Oil the hair regularly, and tie it up in strands wrapped in paper. The hair can grow better this way and is not shed. The paper

Taking Your Yorkie to a Show

wrappers also prevent dogs from chewing on the beard hair when eating. Since the quality and the length of the hair are hereditary, you will want to demonstrate that your dog's hair is long and healthy. In dogs whose hair is not wrapped and put up, the hair automatically breaks off at a certain point, which makes a check of hair length impossible. Wrapping the hair in papers is also practical in the case of male dogs, which lift a leg to urinate. It keeps the hair on the hind legs cleaner.

Please don't confuse this putting up of the hair with putting hair up in curlers. The wrapping is done exclusively to protect the hair. An exhibition Yorkie is not supposed to have curls. The hair must look completely straight after it has been blow-dried. If you know from the outset that you are interested in showing your dog, you should get it used to this procedure from the time it is nine or ten months old. A Yorkie with its hair up in paper wrappers may look weird to the ordinary person, but we can assure you that our Yorkies with their hair up feel just as comfortable as those with their hair down.

If you put your Yorkie's hair up, you will need some additional grooming supplies, available at pet supply stores and mail order companies.

• a wrapping oil, whose basic ingredient is often mink oil, especially manufactured for the grooming of Yorkshire terriers. For a container you can use a spray bottle with a misting nozzle.
• sheets of acid-free paper for wrapping, measuring 7 ½ by 10 inches (19 by 25 cm) and available from specialized pet supply mail order companies. Regular tissue paper damages the hair.
• a special shampoo
• a hair rinse or conditioner that replenishes the skin and hair oils, has an anti-static effect, and adds gloss to the hair
• rubber bands in the proper sizes

How to Go About It

• After you have removed all knots and matted tan-gles and brushed the hair, spray it with the wrapping oil.
• Fold the curling paper in half lengthwise.
• Then lay a strand of hair onto the the paper (see photo on page 56) and fold the paper around it. Get a firm grip on the strand of hair near the skin and on the paper, so that manipulation of the hair won't cause pulling.
• Now fold the paper up in half lengths as many times as seems reasonable for the length of the hair.
• Finally, tie the wrapper in place with a rubber band (not too tight).

The photograph on page 56 shows how the hair should be divided into strands. The hair on the entire body and head should end up in even "packets" on both sides of the part. The wrappers should be checked every day and, if they have been nibbled on or are loose or very dirty, replaced. Ordinarily all the wrappers are replaced with new ones one to three times a week.

Taking Off the Wrappers: On the day of the exhibition, the dog is relieved of the paper wrappers and then bathed and blow-dried (see page 40). To prevent the ends of hair from splitting, it is best to trim the tips from time to time. To get the hair an even length, stand the Yorkie on a table, and cut the hair in a straight line along the the edge of the table. Be sure to hold on to the dog, so it will not fall off the table.

Ear Care

The hair on the upper third of the ears should be shaved (see drawing, page 64). For this we use small battery-operated clippers that are run carefully inside and along the outer edges of the ears. Then we go over the outer edges once more with small scissors. Get the dog used to the clippers slowly. The humming noise may bother it at first.

Other Preparations

To display your Yorkie at a show, you need a carrier that you can turn into a pedestal by draping a velvet cover over it. Your Yorkie should present itself on this stand upright and with a straight back (see drawing, page 64). It should also walk along well on a leash and let the judge handle it to check its bite among other things. Start practicing these things early, from about six months on, if you plan to show your dog more than once or twice. If you make a game of the training, your Yorkie will cooperate enthusiastically.

Preparing a dog for a show can be a lot of work. Please don't be disappointed if the rating your dog receives does not seem commensurate with the trouble you took getting ready.

Useful Literature and Addresses

For Information and Printed Materials:

American Society for the Prevention of Cruelty to
Animals (ASPCA)
    441 East 92nd Street
    New York, New York 10028
American Veterinary Medical Association
    930 North Meacham Road
    Schaumburg, Illinois 60173
Humane Society of the United States
    2100 L Street N.W.
    Washington, DC 20037

International Kennel Clubs:

The American Kennel Club (AKC)
    51 Madison Avenue
    New York, New York 10038
The Kennel Club
    1–4 Clargis Street Picadilly
    London W7Y 8AB
    England
Canadian Kennel Club
    111 Eglington Avenue
    Toronto 12, Ontario
    Canada
Australian National Kennel Council
    Royal Show Grounds
    Ascot Vale
    Victoria
    Australia
Irish Kennel Club
    41 Harcourt Street
    Dublin 2
    Ireland
New Zealand Kennel Club
    P.O. Box 523
    Wellington, 1
    New Zealand

The current Corresponding Secretary for the Yorkshire Terrier Club of America, Inc. is:
    Betty Dullinger
    R.F.D. 2, Box 104
    Kezar Falls, ME 04047
Since new officers are elected periodically, contact the AKC for the latest information.

Books

Alderton, David. *The Dog Care Manual.* Barron's Educational Series, Hauppauge, New York, 1986

Baer, Ted. *Communicating with Your Dog.* Barron's Educational Series, Hauppauge, New York, 1989.

Frye, Fredric. *First Aid for Your Dog.* Barron's Educational Series, Hauppauge, New York, 1987.

Huxham, Mona. *All About the Yorkshire Terrier.* Pelham Books Ltd. London, Great Britain, 1981

Kern, Kerry *The New Terrier Handbook.* Barron's Educational Series, Hauppauge, New York, 1988.

Klever, Ulrich. *The Complete Book of Dog Care.* Barron's Educational Series, Hauppauge, New York, 1989.

Lorenz, Konrad Z. *Man Meets Dog.* Penguin Books, London and New York. 1967.

Smythe, Reginald H. *The Mind of the Dog.* Thomas, Bannerstone House, London, Great Britain, 1961.

Ullmann, Hans-J. *The New Dog Handbook.* Barron's Educational Series, Hauppauge, New York, 1985.

Index

Page references in *italics* indicate color photos

Index

Index

Perfect for Pet Owners!

PET OWNER'S MANUALS

Over 50 illustrations per book (20 or more color photos), 72–80 pp., paperback.

AFRICAN GRAY PARROTS (3773-1)
AMAZON PARROTS (4035-X)
BANTAMS (3687-5)
BEAGLES (3829-0)
BEEKEEPING (4089-9)
BOSTON TERRIERS (1696-3)
BOXERS (4036-8)
CANARIES (4611-0)
CATS (4442-8)
CHINCHILLAS (4037-6)
CHOW-CHOWS (3952-1)
CICHLIDS (4597-1)
COCKATIELS (4610-2)
COCKER SPANIELS (1478-2)
COCKATOOS (4159-3)
COLLIES (1875-3)
CONURES (4880-6)
DACHSHUNDS (1843-5)
DALMATIANS (4605-6)
DISCUS FISH (4669-2)
DOBERMAN PINSCHERS (2999-2)
DOGS (4822-9)
DOVES (1855-9)
DWARF RABBITS (1352-2)
ENGLISH SPRINGER SPANIELS (1778-1)
FEEDING AND SHELTERING BACKYARD
    BIRDS (4252-2)
FEEDING AND SHELTERING EUROPEAN
    BIRDS (2858-9)
FERRETS (2976-3)
GERBILS (3725-1)
GERMAN SHEPHERDS (2982-8)
GOLDEN RETRIEVERS (3793-6)
GOLDFISH (2975-5)
GOULDIAN FINCHES (4523-8)
GREAT DANES (1418-9)
GUINEA PIGS (4612-9)
GUPPIES, MOLLIES, AND PLATTIES (1497-9)
HAMSTERS (4439-8)
IRISH SETTERS (4663-3)
KEESHONDEN (1560-6)
KILLIFISH (4475-4)
LABRADOR RETRIEVERS (3792-8)
LHASA APSOS (3950-5)
LIZARDS IN THE TERRARIUM (3925-4)
LONGHAIRED CATS (2803-1)
LONG-TAILED PARAKEETS (1351-4)

LORIES AND LORIKEETS (1567-3)
LOVEBIRDS (3726-X)
MACAWS (4768-0)
MICE (2921-6)
MUTTS (4126-7)
MYNAHS (3688-3)
PARAKEETS (4437-1)
PARROTS (4823-7)
PERSIAN CATS (4405-3)
PIGEONS (4044-9)
POMERANIANS (4670-6)
PONIES (2856-2)
POODLES (2812-0)
POT BELLIES AND OTHER MINIATURE PIGS
    (1356-5)
PUGS (1824-9)
RABBITS (4440-1)
RATS (4535-1)
ROTTWEILERS (1183-6)
SCHNAUZERS (3949-1)
SCOTTISH FOLD CATS (4999-3)
SHAR-PEI (4334-2)
SHEEP (4091-0)
SHETLAND SHEEPDOGS (4264-6)
SHIH TZUS (4524-6)
SIAMESE CATS (4764-4)
SIBERIAN HUSKIES (4265-4)
SMALL DOGS (1951-2)
SNAKES (2813-9)
SPANIELS (2424-9)
TROPICAL FISH (4700-1)
TURTLES (4702-8)
WEST HIGHLAND WHITE TERRIERS (1950-4)
YORKSHIRE TERRIERS (4406-1)
ZEBRA FINCHES (3497-X)

NEW PET HANDBOOKS

Detailed, illustrated profiles (40–60 color photos), 144 pp., paperback.

NEW AQUARIUM FISH HANDBOOK (3682-4)
NEW AUSTRALIAN PARAKEET
    HANDBOOK (4739-7)
NEW BIRD HANDBOOK (4157-7)
NEW CANARY HANDBOOK (4879-2)
NEW CAT HANDBOOK (2922-4)
NEW COCKATIEL HANDBOOK (4201-8)
NEW DOG HANDBOOK (2857-0)
NEW DUCK HANDBOOK (4088-0)
NEW FINCH HANDBOOK (2859-7)
NEW GOAT HANDBOOK (4090-2)

NEW PARAKEET HANDBOOK (2985-2)
NEW PARROT HANDBOOK (3729-4)
NEW RABBIT HANDBOOK (4202-6)
NEW SALTWATER AQUARIUM
    HANDBOOK (4482-7)
NEW SOFTBILL HANDBOOK (4075-9)
NEW TERRIER HANDBOOK (3951-3)

REFERENCE BOOKS

Comprehensive, lavishly illustrated references (60–300 color photos), 136–176 pp., hardcover & paperback.

AQUARIUM FISH (1350-6)
AQUARIUM FISH BREEDING (4474-6)
AQUARIUM FISH SURVIVAL MANUAL
    (5686-8)
AQUARIUM PLANTS MANUAL (1687-4)
BEFORE YOU BUY THAT PUPPY (1750-1)
BEST PET NAME BOOK EVER, THE
    (4258-1)
CARING FOR YOUR SICK CAT (1726-9)
CAT CARE MANUAL (5765-1)
CIVILIZING YOUR PUPPY (4953-5)
COMMUNICATING WITH YOUR DOG
    (4203-4)
COMPLETE BOOK OF BUDGERIGARS
    (6059-8)
COMPLETE BOOK OF CAT CARE (4613-7)
COMPLETE BOOK OF DOG CARE (4158-5)
COMPLETE BOOK OF PARROTS (5971-9)
DOG CARE MANUAL (5764-3)
FEEDING YOUR PET BIRD (1521-3)
GOLDFISH AND ORNAMENTAL CARP
    (9286-4)
GUIDE TO A WELL BEHAVED CAT
    (1476-6)
GUIDE TO HOME PET GROOMING
    (4298-0)
HEALTHY DOG, HAPPY DOG (1842-7)
HOP TO IT: A Guide to Training Your Pet Rabbit
    (4551-3)
HORSE CARE MANUAL (1133-3)
HOW TO TALK TO YOUR CAT (1749-8)
HOW TO TEACH YOUR OLD DOG
    NEW TRICKS (4544-0)
LABYRINTH FISH (5635-3)
MACAWS (9037-3)
NONVENOMOUS SNAKES (5632-9)
WATER PLANTS IN THE AQUARIUM (3926-2)

Barron's Educational Series, Inc. • 250 Wireless Blvd., Hauppauge, NY 11788
Call toll-free: 1-800-645-3476 • In Canada: Georgetown Book Warehouse
34 Armstrong Ave., Georgetown, Ont. L7G 4R9 • Call toll-free: 1-800-247-7160
ISBN prefix: 0-8120 • Order from your favorite book or pet store